PREACHING
THROUGH THE
APOCALYPSE
Sermons from Revelation

PREACHING THROUGH THE APOCALYPSE

Sermons from Revelation

Edited with Introductions

by

Cornish R. Rogers
and Joseph R. Jeter, Jr.

Chalice Press®
St. Louis, Missouri

All scripture quotations, unless otherwise indicated, are from the *New Revised Standard Version Bible*, copyright 1989, Division of Christian Education of the National Council of the Churches of Christ in the USA. Used by permission.

Those quotations marked RSV are from the *Revised Standard Version* of the Bible, copyrighted 1946, 1952, © 1971, 1973.

Those quotations marked NEB are from *The New English Bible*, © 1976. The Delegates of the Oxford University Press, Inc., and the Syndics of the Cambridge University Press, 1961, 1970. Reprinted by permission.

Cover design: Michael A. Dominguez

Cover Illustration by Dhimitri Zonia
    based on a drawing by Albrecht Dürer

Library of Congress Cataloging–in–Publication Data

Preaching through the Apocalypse : sermons from Revelation / edited with introductions by Cornish R. Rogers and Joseph R. Jeter, Jr. Includes bibliographical references.
ISBN 0-8272 -2944-5
1. Bible. N.T. Revelation—Sermons. 2. Sermons, American.
I. Rogers, Cornish R.   II. Jeter, Joseph R.
BS2825.4.P74 1992   252   92-26072

Printed in the United States of America

Contents

INTRODUCTION

The twenty-first century approaches. Historically, interest in the book of Revelation rises toward the end of a century. Century-end brings with it feelings of insecurity and displacement that are often hospitable to apocalyptic thought. And rising apocalypticism brings renewed interest in and fascination with its most famous literary example: the biblical book of Revelation. The century-end approaching will surely follow this trend. We further believe that this interest will be even more acute than usual this time because of three additional facts. First, this will be the first century-end in history to be lived under the threats of nuclear and environmental holocaust. The "end of time," a concept heretofore relegated to the domain of God alone, may now be only a push of a button or a disappearing ozone layer away. Second, this time we are approaching not only the end of a century but also the end of a millennium! Millennialism will be abroad in the land. Members of the Jesus Seminar, a collection of biblical scholars, warned in a recent meeting that "the time is ripe for prophets of doom."[1] Third, the recent war in the Persian Gulf became the catalyst for considerable apocalyptic fervor in this country. One national columnist remarked: "On radio shows, in churches, in seminaries—especially among conservative evangelicals—you hear eschatological language: the Antichrist, 666, the millennium, the Rapture."[2] Another prominent pastor exclaimed that the war was "a dress rehearsal for Armageddon."[3] And John Walvoord's book entitled *Armageddon, Oil and the Middle East Crisis* sold over a million copies in a very short time.[4] For all these reasons interest in the book of Revelation may be reaching an all-time high. There may well be more sermons preached out of Revelation in the next ten years than there have been in the last hundred or more.

This book has been written because of our fear that many of those sermons are going to be bad and our conviction that they need not be so. Revelation has important messages for our time, but many preachers shy away from the text for a variety of reasons: strange theology, bizarre imagery, difficult structure, unusual language, and so forth. Through theory and example we want to consider the preaching values present in the book and various homiletical approaches to the text.

That this is primarily a book of sermons, and not just a book about preaching sermons, reflects our "bicycle-riding" approach to the task of preaching. It is one thing to read a book on bicycle riding that discusses mechanics, aerodynamics, and so forth. It is quite another to get on a bicycle and begin pedaling, with the terror and exhilaration that attend that experience. The same holds true with preaching.

We have approached many of the very best preachers known to us: pastors and professors, Americans and non-Americans, blacks and whites, men and women, preachers from various theological and denominational backgrounds, and put the same challenge to all of them: struggle with the text, structure and preach the word you find there for the people given into your care, and send us your best work. The result is eighteen sermons grounded in every major section of John's work, together with a "prelude" by James Forbes that addresses the task of preaching on the verge of the new millennium, and a "postlude" by Jaroslav Vajda, that hymns the ultimate glory of God. Two of the sermons are our own for which we beg the reader's indulgence. The sermons range from the discursive to the poetic, from the expository to the thematic, from the irenic to the confrontational, from the pain-wracked to the joy-filled. But they all have this in common: they attempt to engage seriously both John's text and the contemporary reader/hearer.

While all the sermons in this book come from those who claim the office of preacher, more representatives of the academy than the parish are present. The main reason for this is that most of the pastors from whom we sought sermons declined the invitation. One such pastor, one of America's greatest preachers, spoke for many when he wrote, "I am one of those who need to buy your volume rather than contribute to it, for I have done very little preaching from Revelation." This tends to confirm that there is not much grain in the storehouse out there. While a disappointment, it heightened our sense of the need for this project and brought much rejoicing in the sermons that were forthcoming.

The sermons are preceded by two introductory pieces. The first is by Rogers and deals with preaching values in the book of Revelation, gleaned from years of teaching seminary courses and preaching in black and white churches on this continent and in Africa. What does the book have to offer the people of the 1990s? The second is by Jeter and considers homiletical approaches to preaching Revelation texts, approaches tried by fire in classroom, workshop, and pulpit. We are grateful to all our preachers for their hard, faithful work and their splendid response to the high demands of the preacher's office. We also wish to acknowledge the counsel and encouragement of Dr. M. Eugene Boring, professor of New Testament at Brite Divinity School. His knowledge and help were critical to this project.

Our fondest hope is that this book may lead preachers who might otherwise avoid Revelation to give John's book the serious consideration it deserves and help them find ways to preach the significant word that Revelation contains for people living in the waning days of the twentieth century, looking toward the new millennium that is aborning.

Cornish R. Rogers
Joseph R. Jeter, Jr.

Notes

¹Don Lattin, "Time Is Ripe for Prophets of Doom, Group Warns," *San Francisco Chronicle*, 2 March 1992, A3.

²Barbara Reynolds, "From the Heart," *USA Today*, 21 September 1990, 11.

³Mike Evans, quoted in the *Fort Worth Star-Telegram*, 12 January 1991, E7.

⁴See "The War Is Over; What's Next," *Christian Retailing*, 15 April 1991, 13.

Preaching Values in the Book of Revelation

Cornish R. Rogers

What does the book of Revelation say? What are its values for preaching in these latter days of the twentieth century? In this chapter we suggest three things: a way of approaching apocalyptic thought as *creative negativity*; seeing the call of Revelation to be faithful to God and the promise of Revelation to be vindication in Christ for those who are faithful; and the power and challenge of Revelation's images to *unmask appearances*, to unveil the truth about the world and ourselves.

✳ ✳ ✳

When I began teaching a course entitled "Preaching Values in the Book of Revelation," I got some funny, evasive looks from a few members of the Bible faculty. It was not until much later, after having taught it twice, that I was informed by the dean that some questions had been raised about my qualifications to teach the course since I was obviously not trained as a biblical scholar. When I replied that the course was not intended to be a "Bible" course but a course in preaching, he expressed his full support but wanted me to know that some of the Bible faculty were uneasy about it. Their uneasiness stemmed from the unsettled place of Revelation in the opinions of the scholars.

One ministerial colleague confessed, "I can't figure it out, so I leave it alone." Another one said to me sympathetically, "If I were an oppressed minority, I would love the book of Revelation," implying that, not being a minority person, he had no use for it.

1

Aversion to Revelation goes back to the early church and has been especially strong since the historical-critical method of Bible study came into vogue. New Testament scholar Amos Wilder reported that, when he chose to write his doctoral dissertation on eschatology and ethics in 1929, he received a letter from Walter Lowrie:

> For myself I have serious counsel to give you. If you would have a long life and would see good days, keep mum on the subject of eschatology…a subject which is highly dangerous in these days. Your teachers give you good advice: eschatology is a subject which the good and the great conspire to shun.[1]

While there may be a subtle difference between *eschatology* and *apocalyptic*, the terms are often used interchangeably. But, according to Karl Rahner: "to extrapolate from the present into the future is eschatology, to interpolate from the future into the present is apocalyptic."[2]

Eschatology in this view, then, is *futurum*: the becoming of the present; apocalyptic is *adventus*: the coming of the future. Eschatology tends toward an evolutionary monism while apocalyptic embraces a revolutionary dualism. A simplistic way of expressing the difference is that eschatology leads to reform while apocalyptic leads to revolution. "Christians," says Jürgen Moltmann, "are joyous revolutionaries." Recognizing apocalyptic as a central New Testament genre, Ernest Kasemann contends that "Apocalyptic is the mother of Christian Theology." David Tracy considers apocalyptic a corrective to the New Testament in that it challenges a private understanding of the Gospels. It is a reminder of the public, political, and historical character of Christian self-understanding, and of the privileged place of the poor, the oppressed, and those who suffer. And not only does it challenge the living to remember the dead, but also reminds the wise and orderly that the ultimate power ordering the cosmos is essentially unfathomable.[3]

Because of its revolutionary character, apocalyptic has a negative cast to it, albeit a *creative negativity*. The New Creation is born through the negation of the old, and is not its mere replacement."[4] In the book of Revelation, the demonic is used to reveal Christ, just as in the Gospels, it is the demon-possessed who are able to recognize Jesus.

The role of the diabolic may be to destroy pride in a misconceived virtue. It is revealing that a Russian physician said at an international conference of physicians in 1988:

In the Apocalypse there are the following words: "And there fell a great star from Heaven...and the name of the star is called Wormwood...and the waters became wormwood and many died of the waters because they were made bitter." *The Ukrainian word for wormwood is Chernobyl.* Where did the Chernobyl wormwood star come from? I am sure it was sent to us from the 21st Century as a menacing sign, demanding us to think over the very survival of our civilization before it is too late.[5]

So, in spite of the imprecations of some mainline clergy and scholars, Revelation is enjoying an enormous popularity in the religious imagination of ordinary people in our nation and around the world. As the end of the millennium nears, the book's dire judgments seem to burn more brightly than before. TV evangelists and evangelical preachers everywhere are preaching with great effect their fundamentalistic interpretation of the book. Lay persons are asking more questions about the future of the world as a result of the book's apparent disturbing message. And mainline denominational preachers have conspired to shun the book entirely with an awesome display of silence—a silence admittedly imposed by fear that the book is not sufficiently Christian to be intelligible.

But Revelation is a book whose time has come, and we ignore its preaching message at our own peril. Not only are we nearing the end of a Christian millennium when "end time" interests increase, but we are made more aware of the dangerous possibilities inherent in the sustained conflict in the Middle East between Jew and Arab in the vicinity of Armageddon and other places identified in the book. With the advent of nuclear power, we can actually imagine the possibility of the world coming to an end in our lifetime. Already we have witnessed massive surd evils, like the Jewish holocaust and the Jonestown massacre, just to mention two, which serve to prefigure an even more apocalyptic future triggered by evil people. Prominent public officials, like Ronald Reagan and James Watt, have lent their prestige to give legitimacy to a literalistic view of the book.

But it is this age's addiction to picture imagery, fueled by television, interplanetary travel, and far-out science fiction that increases the ability to imagine the lurid images, grotesque figures, violent conflict, and interstellar action described in the book. It is, in a word, great theater! And more than drama, it is musical drama!

We have been forced through world events and a lingering *Pax Americana* to adopt a global view of things. Revelation projects a universal view of history—a view that includes all peoples and all times, even the heavens. It is the preeminent book of the Bible that breaks down the barrier between humans and nature, introducing an ecological consciousness and a cosmic scope of existence. The forces of both good and evil are supported by Nature and its processes.

So despite the hesitation of some, present-day preachers *must* deal with Revelation. It is being preached to more than minorities and Third World congregations. White people of all classes are being taunted, threatened, and inspired by its "creative negativities" also. While there are many difficult and unintelligible portions of the book still to be unveiled by the scholars, there is enough of the saving gospel of Jesus Christ in it for all preachers to proclaim the gospel through it.

The need for the gospel to be preached from this book is crucial because the approach of most fundamentalist preachers is to preach not the gospel, but a message of fear and dire judgment lacking in the positive dimensions of the gospel. Missing in much of present preaching of the Apocalypse is

> the phase of miraculous renovation and that world affirmation which has gone through the experience of world negation....The full apocalyptic scenario should include salvation as well as judgment, the new-age as well as the old.[6]

* * *

The pastoral letter we know as the book of Revelation was written by a Christian prophet named John who is otherwise unknown to us.[7] It is generally agreed that Revelation was written by John to a group of beleaguered Christians near the end of the first century C.E., urging them to hold on to their faith in the face of severe oppression by the Roman authorities, who insisted that they include the Roman emperor as one of the Gods they must worship. It was written to remind them of the commandment: "thou shalt have no other Gods before me," the Judeo-Christian warning against idolatry. The warning against idolatry runs throughout the book. Even when God's angels come to the aid of the Elect, they warn the Elect not to worship them, but to worship only God. The warning against idolatry connects the Old Testament Exodus experience with the early church by connecting God's deliverance of the Jews from Egypt with the promise that God will deliver them, too, if they refrain from worshiping any "graven images," such as that of the Roman emperor. Many images from the Exodus populate the book.

Revelation is a call to be faithful to God and to be assured that help from on high is on the way through Jesus Christ, the sacrificial conquering lamb, who has become God's instrument in establishing God's reign on earth. The book's intention is not to scare, but to assure that God's justice will be done on behalf of the faithful who suffer because of their faithfulness. As strange as it may appear from a superficial reading, the book is a priestly one designed to give comfort. Even those who suffer unto death are promised eventual resurrection in the last days when the new city of God is established.

Although the book may be structured according to ancient traditions for apocalyptic literature, it lucidly illustrates through its interludes the paradoxical Christian lifestyle of alternation between suffering and joy. One reads of the horrible unrelieved suffering of the saints only to come to an interlude of joyful worship and celebration of the coming victory of the forces of good! Then follows more terrible portents and suffering that are almost unbearable when another interlude of worship, reassurance, and celebration appears. The rhythm of suffering and joy constitutes the lifestyle of the Christian. The joy produces juices that enable one to endure the suffering to come. It opens the door for "otherworldly joys" to spill over into this world. As long as one takes the long view, one can always rejoice even in tribulation; for the end time—that glorious time when the New Jerusalem comes down from God out of heaven like a bride adorned for her husband—is assured. It is a time of vindication.

It has been said that the Apocalypse is a representation of the way the world looks after the ego has disappeared. Perhaps its fascination lies in its unveiled truth about ourselves. The images of Revelation are grotesque perhaps because we are blinded by our egos. Jacques Maritain is reported to have said about Picasso: "His distorted faces are perhaps our true likenesses, when we are seen by the angels."[8] Like Picasso, Revelation paints in lurid cartoon images in order to evoke the true likeness of crisis reality. It is at the gut level that the book communicates truth. It is more than cartoon, more than poetic imagery; it is the stuff of which dreams are made. Images are conjured up to fit feelings. "Will has trouble sleeping, yet is fascinated by his dreams. He tells Lil: 'My dreams seem to know more than I know.'"[9] Images appear to have a life of their own. They appear in one form and are transformed into another form. They are not governed by reason but by symbol. The symbols are derived from an ancient archetypal system that was once consciously understood but has been lost through the mists of history.

"As silently as a mirror is believed, realities plunge in silence by."[10] Those realities, or images, are the votive force of the book. Their appropriation conveys more than what the text says. Isadora Duncan is said to have remarked, when asked what one of her dances meant, "If I could tell you, I would not have to dance it."[11] Wendy Doniger O'Flaherty, in her book, *Dreams, Illusions and Other Realities*, writes that if the Hindu storyteller "sets out to tell a tale of revelation, he may describe events that peel back the physical veil to reveal another, more mystical reality that was always there but not recognized."[12] The images created by the wedding of the text with the imagination of the reader/hearer become what James Sanders called "mirrors of identity rather than models of morality." That, he maintains, is the proper hermeneutical approach to the Scriptures.[13] All Scripture, like Revelation, is an unmasking of appearances, a revealing of ultimate truth behind present reality. Even for Dante, the journey up Mount Purgatory in *The Divine Comedy* was a way of seeing his essential self stripped of all pretensions. And his use of terror was for purification, not penalty. Terror, in Revelation also, is purgative, not penal, in its intended effect.

The structure of Revelation is elaborate and probably patterned after the book of Ezekiel. It has an upstairs/downstairs quality about it: one has to be aware of what is taking place in heaven and what is taking place on earth. It is difficult to assess the time sequences; time appears to be both vertical and horizontal, swinging on an axis. One must read the book with a wide-angle lens, or more aptly, with a split-screen lens. But in the order of their reportage, the following chronology occurs:

Chapter I	The Vision of Christ by John of Patmos
II and III	Letters to the Churches
IV and V	Preparatory Visions
VI to XVI	Seven Seals, Trumpets, Mystic Signs, Bowls. (Interludes are usually just before the seventh vision, and introduce the next cycle.)
XVII to XIX	Final Destruction of Babylon
XX	Thousand-year Reign and Last Judgment
XXI and XXII	New Jerusalem

The uniqueness of Revelation is its *visions*, or images. They appear to have lives of their own outside the context of the book.

Christ is depicted as exalted and as conquering and vengeful. Evil is depicted as a dragon, as a beast, and as a woman astride a beast. Several images of negativity (seals, trumpets, the harvest of God's vengeance, the bowls of wrath, Armageddon) are matched by images of order and integration (worship in the Heavenly Court, New Jerusalem). Feminine images, both negative and positive, include Jezebel, The woman clothed with the sun, the woman on the scarlet beast, and the New Jerusalem as a bride.

A striking parallel of good and evil images emerges from the book. The images project a mirror world of good and evil, images that look suspiciously like each other unless one looks closely. There is the Holy Trinity of God, the Lamb, and the bride; and the unholy Trinity of the dragon (Satan), the beast, and the whore. There are two beasts (one is later called a false prophet) and two prophets, all of whom have miraculous powers. Both the beasts and the prophets reign for forty-two months, 1260 days. There is a seal of the beast and a seal of the Elect, as well as marks of slaughter on both the beast and the Lamb. It is as if evil tries to beguile us into thinking it is the good. It reminds us that the lure of goodness and the lure of evil are almost equally attractive.

Through the power of its images, Revelation has found an enduring place in the imagination of Western history and culture. Artists, musicians, and writers have incorporated its images into the works of their imagination. If all copies of the book were destroyed tomorrow, its essential message would live on in Western art, music, and literature. One needs only to visit Chartres and other European cathedrals to experience an architecture patterned after the description of the New Jerusalem, or listen to the triumphant strains of Handel's *Hallelujah Chorus* to sense the exaltation over the marriage of the Lamb. Western literature is replete with allusions to the lurid scenes in Revelation. The book enjoys popularity even among non-Christians, many of whom regard it as their favorite book of the Bible.

What makes the book so compelling is a language that combines disclosure with ecstasy. "The language of the apocalyptist is an acclamation that echoes and continues the event, the *miraculum*. It is reflexive, not reflective....The language is part of the happening."[14] The language then actually becomes a participant in the enjoyment of the disclosure! But in order for that disclosure to be enjoyed, one must be sensitive and aware of analogous parallels in the present situations. That is why the book invites interpretations that are risky and often faulty, unless one struggles to read the signs of the times from a broad and balanced gospel perspective.

Isak Dineson has maintained that any sorrow or suffering can be borne provided it can be put into a story. Revelation is such a story. It is a story of the future about to break into a suffering, sorrowful present. Because of the secularization of our culture, the future, said Harvey Cox in a recent speech, "is the only dimension in which the transcendent can operate; so the future becomes the source of freedom, and imagination becomes the necessary sensibility for hope." Revelation says more. It promises that the future belongs not to the beasts, but the lambs. And listen to the lambs! We must preach the lambs' song.

Notes

[1]Amos N. Wilder, *Jesus' Parables and the War of Myths* (Philadelphia: Fortress, 1982), p. 25.

[2]Karl Rahner, cited by Carl Braaten, *Christ and Counter-Christ* (Philadelphia: Fortress, 1927), p. 9.

[3]David Tracy, *The Analogical Imagination* (New York: Crossroad, 1981), pp. 265ff.

[4]Braaten, *Christ and Counter-Christ*, p. 18.

[5]From a speech by Dr. Yuri Stscherbak, a physician from Kiev, given on 13 October 1988 during the Congress of International Physicians for the Prevention of Nuclear War.

[6]Wilder, *Jesus' Parables and the War of Myths*, p. 167.

[7]See M. Eugene Boring, *Revelation, Interpretation: A Bible Commentary for Teaching and Preaching* (Louisville: John Knox Press, 1989), p. 34.

[8]Hearsay. Source unknown.

[9]A. G. Mojtabai, cited in *Christian Information Service*, 30 Oct 1982, p. 4.

[10]Hart Crane, "White Buildings," in *Collected Poems of Hart Crane* (New York: Liveright, 1946), p. 61.

[11]Source unknown.

[12]Wendy Doniger O'Flaherty, *Dreams, Illusions and Other Realities* (Chicago: Univ. of Chicago Press, 1984), p. 3.

[13]James A. Sanders, *God Has a Story, Too* (Philadelphia: Fortress, 1979), p. 134.

[14]Wilder, *Jesus' Parables and the War of Myths*, p. 162.

Revelation-Based Preaching: Homiletical Approaches

Joseph R. Jeter, Jr.

"I never touch the book of Revelation except for funerals. Too weird. Too dangerous." The preacher who said that could have spoken for many. Relatively few preachers are comfortable with Revelation-based sermons. Those who make most frequent use of Revelation tend to operate within dispensationalist systems that see Revelation as predicting current or future events. For example, I was once at worship in Los Angeles when the service was interrupted by a self-styled prophet who proclaimed that Ronald Wilson Reagan was the Antichrist. Her reasoning was that the sum of the numerical value of the letters of his name combined to form the number 666, placing him under the "mark of the beast" in Revelation 13. Others have recently seen Mikhail Gorbachev's birthmark as the mark of the beast, considerably complicating the issue. And the locale of the recent war in the Middle East, so "near" to Armageddon, has fueled the fires of "end time" talk.

If one rejects that mode of interpretation, as we must, then how *does* one move from the ancient book of Revelation to a word both faithful to the text and significant for the lives of twentieth-century-end hearers? Many of the values, themes, truths, and theological issues of the Apocalypse have been raised in the preceding chapter. Our concern here is with the question of how we preach them. Canon and content may provide the impetus that draws us into the text. But how then do we get out of it? How do we get back to our time with a message? What does good Revelation-based preaching look and sound like?

9

The hermeneutical and homiletical questions are next on our agenda, but a word of caution is first in order. Revelation has shown itself to be good meat for Bible study. People in these memorial times have also shown themselves to be interested in digging into this fascinating book. However, we need to remember—and I differ with Bonhoeffer here—that, although much Bible study is involved in preaching, preaching is not Bible study. Preaching is proclamation. It is, in the words of Ian Maclaren, the attempt to "speak a good word for Jesus Christ."[1] Because Revelation comes to us wrapped in a world view and language so alien to our own time, many responsible preachers see a good deal of introduction and background as necessary. While this is commendable, the danger is that so much time may be spent in table-setting that the meal never gets served. I have heard many Revelation-based sermons that foundered in the shallow waters of explanatory material.

The historical context of Revelation appropriate to interpreting the text can be briefly, dramatically retold as part of the sermon. But a sermon that spends eighteen minutes explaining the difference between apocalyptic and nonapocalyptic literature and then two minutes trying to make some contemporary "point" about a passage from Revelation is a sermon likely to frustrate preacher and listener alike. Background material needs to be kept to a minimum and needs to serve the purpose for which the sermon is preached.

Now, to the sermon. The remainder of this chapter suggests that preaching from Revelation invites us to:

a. Explore the use of symbol and metaphor in our preaching.
b. Consider how narrative texts may lend themselves to narrative sermons.
c. Imaginatively reconstruct ancient images into pictures that people today can see.
d. Consider Revelation's natural affinity to experiences of worship.
e. Confront Revelation's tensions homiletically.
f. Test our understanding of God's power and promises in a post-Holocaust world.

These invitations emerge from a multi-faceted approach to the text, taking into account current critical concerns. Recent studies of apocalyptic literature in general and the book of Revelation in particular have tended to focus upon three areas crucial to interpreting and preaching from such texts. The areas have been variously labeled and sometimes blur into one another, but they have most commonly been designated form, function, and content.[2] Oversimplifying, *form* has to do with the manner in which the text comes to us, *function* with the purpose of the text then and now, and *content* with what the text says. Using these categories, let us look at the task of preaching from Revelation.

Form

There is growing concern among homileticians that we take seriously the form in which the text comes to us as we prepare our sermons. Does it mean anything for the shape and substance of the sermon that the text we have before us is saga, parable, miracle story, or apocalypse? For much of the Bible, the admonition to let the form of the text inform the shape of the sermon is, though not easy, manageable. Most of us have the tools for working with familiar genres. But when we come to the book of Revelation, we find a different thing altogether. Preaching in the western world has by and large followed a logical, categorical approach in lock step. It has been straightforward, prosaic, "call a spade a spade" preaching. It has also, with blessed exceptions, been wooden and dull. But since it has been our way, we are uncomfortable with literature like John's Revelation, in which he calls a spade a pitchfork.

The first suggestion, then, is that the preacher can benefit from the study of the literary genre of Revelation itself. What is the genre of Revelation? It is a pastoral letter that exhibits many of the characteristics of apocalyptic literature. Some of those characteristics—otherworldly journeys, mediating angels, and so forth—may not be frequently useful to the preacher. As Austin Farrer has suggested, it is vain to tell people to imagine in ways that they find unimaginable.[3] But there are some aspects of this apocalyptic letter that are compellingly useful. I wish to focus here upon the fact that the letter comes to us largely as narrative, with language that is highly symbolic and evocative.

1. Symbolic Narrative

A narrative text or sermon, according to Eugene Lowry, is one that moves from disequilibrium through escalation to reversal and denouement.[4] On the surface Revelation surely qualifies. Things are bad. They are going to get worse. But eventually the beast will be cast down and God's reign established. That the end, according to John, is already determined and has been since the beginning of time may rob the narrative of some of its literary tension, but none of its power, since this is an end that has not yet come and that some days seems further away then ever. The Revelation narrative worked by allowing people in great distress to hear and experience the promise of God's future action on their behalf. It offers us a window through which people in trouble today can have their problems named and hear the encouragement to faithfulness and the promise of that hope beyond human hope that is found in God.

The narrative nature of Revelation is made more complex, and more interesting, in that it comes to us largely written in symbolic language. There is no question that this is a problem for preacher and people alike, one that revolves around our inability to function on a symbolic level. Imagine a communion service in a typical suburban church on a Sunday morning. The liturgy is intoned, the elements are distributed, and suddenly the parishioners discover real human flesh on the paten and real human blood in the chalice. There would, I suppose, be much gagging, wailing, and gnashing of teeth. It is not flesh and blood on the table, it is bread and wine. But many, who cannot function on a symbolic level, have gone through no end of theo-linguistic contortions to satisfy their need for this to literally be Christ's body and blood and not "merely" symbolic of them.

Consider these statements by John J. Collins:

> Apocalyptic literature was not governed by the principles of Aristotelian logic but was closer to the poetic nature of myth....The apocalyptic literature provides a rather clear example of language that is expressive rather than referential, symbolic rather than factual.[5]

Are there preaching occasions that call for sermons like that? More poetic than logical, feeling-based rather than fact-based, pictorial rather than propositional? Some biblical stories can be related with the parenetic tag "go and do likewise" or "go and do not do likewise." Revelation, as mentioned, tends to resist that kind of one-to-one correspondence. So do many themes and problems we encounter in our preaching ministries. Concepts like heaven and love are not easily defined. Events like tragedies as well as unexplainable good fortune are not easily categorized. Sometimes in preaching a story is better than a definition, a picture better than a proposition.

For example, in Revelation 15, a sort of prelude to the bowls of wrath, we find the Song of the Lamb. The song is introduced this way: "And I saw what appeared to be a sea of glass...." Peace activist Daniel Berrigan, sitting in the Alexandria, Virginia, city jail, meditated upon this text. Later he would write a book about it, in which he said:

> The phrase intrigued, teased, puzzled me. Since boyhood I have loved the sea, gotten lost (and found) by the sea, recouped my spirit there, listened and learned there, at times even been reborn there. I have known all its moods and changes....
>
> But one thing I have never known, and I doubt indeed whether such a thing exists at all, this side of the veil. Namely, the marvel described by Revelation as the setting for the Prayer of the Lamb: a "sea of glass." That, I said to myself, will bear more imagining. For it must have been imagined in order to exist at all.[6]

Berrigan's book has an interesting structure. He moves through the Song of the Lamb verse by verse and thought by thought. The method is classical exposition. This is what it meant. This is what it means. The language is crisp, the argument compelling. But when it comes to John's setting for the prayer, the landscape—or better, seascape—of the text, Berrigan does not say, "What we have here is a metaphor for tranquillity" or even "This is surely here to stand in contrast to the chaotic waters of the creation story or perhaps to bring to mind the Red Sea of the Exodus." He says, rather, "I want to tell you a story."

And then he does, a story about a restless sea unleashed by the Creator against sin and then, its damage done and point made, receding until it becomes as smooth as glass.

> The waters which had advanced fierce, warlike and stealthy, turned about and crept back on all sides from the mountain. They were like warriors whose mission is over....Then the Creator said to the Waters: "You have tasted your great power. You have been the lowliest, then mightiest of all. You must now dwell in the middle ground. I promise you, never again will you be humiliated among creatures. Dwell now at peace with the world."[7]

Berrigan is here writing the way John wrote. Images like the "sea of glass" are weak, insipid things if treated as propositions alone. As Berrigan says, a literal sea of glass defies credulity and, in truth, would be a pretty stupid-looking thing. But treated as the symbol that it is, and wrapped in a creative narrative, the sea of glass becomes a powerful metaphor for a world-made-right-at-last, a setting where the Song of the Lamb can really be experienced. Now, Berrigan was writing a book, not preaching a sermon, but the use of narratives or symbols in the place of neutral explanatory material can work wonderfully in sermons as well.

2. Evocative Language

The question of form raises another pertinent concern, which could also be considered under the questions of function or content. This is the fact that apocalyptic texts not only differ from other garden-variety narratives in the amount of symbolism involved, but also in that the language is highly evocative. The reader/listener is no passive recipient, but an active participant. Because "the images of apocalypses are somewhat opaque,...the hearers must participate in order to understand and apply them."[8]

Consider G. A. Studdert-Kennedy's *The Wicket Gate,* from 1929. His stated concern in the book was to feed people the good plain bread of religion. But he knew that since the end of World War I the world had changed. The old Victorian individualism had passed away and people felt lost. The familiar nineteenth-century systems and categories had faded away before them. Searching for a way to help people find their way through the spiritual and psychological darkness, he happened upon the image that shaped his book, from Bunyun's *Pilgrim's Progress.*[9] At one point therein Pilgrim was lost, cried out "What shall I do?" and wanted to run, but did not know which way to go.

> Then said Evangelist, pointing with his finger over a very wide field, "Do you see yonder wicket gate?" The man said "No." Then said the other, "Do you see yonder shining light?" He said, "I think I do." Then said Evangelist, "Keep that light in your eye, and go up directly thereto: so shalt thou see the gate; at which when thou knockest, it shalt be told thee what thou shalt do.[10]

Studdert-Kennedy's world and its needs seem almost as far from ours as that of John, the author of Revelation. But this scene from Bunyun is very helpful. It goes like this: before you can know what to do, you must knock on the gate; in order to knock on the gate, you must simply follow the light. There are times when what is needful in a sermon is not the logical delineation of the answer to the problem or even the action that must be taken so as to obtain the answer. What may be helpful is a sermon that simply points the way toward the landscape or playing field where the answer may be encountered and calls people to come and be problem solvers.

I once heard a lecture on Rembrandt in which the lecturer admonished us: "When looking at a Rembrandt, always follow the light."[11] We sometimes need sermons painted on a word canvas that invite that instruction, pictures that will provide impetus, setting and trajectory for the Christian journey. For example, there are times when "Seek ye first the kingdom of God and God's righteousness, and all these things shall be yours as well" and "First go and be reconciled with your brother or sister; then come and make your offering" will preach on their own. But there are other times when these truths have a neutral one-dimensional quality about them that is not compelling. Then they need to be brush-stroked onto a two-dimensional canvas (the wicket gate) or recounted in a three-dimensional narrative (the sea of glass) that will not just transmit the truth, but colorcast it, not just instruct the listener, but invite the listener into its world.

Revelation works like that. Revelation offers us images that cannot be reduced to propositions, confessions that cannot be treated as objective reports, and a rhetorical matrix in which the word pictures portray events that are synchronic rather than diachronic. That is, they happen all at once rather than in an orderly sequence. That which needs saying can only be suggested, evoked, pointed to, like Bunyun's wicket gate. In Eugene Boring's words, "apocalyptic language functions to say what it cannot quite say, but must say."[12] To preach from Revelation, as John Lurvey puts it, we must "attractively project images that are more than eloquence can bear."[13] And this is done with evocative intent: to call the listener to action.

We may not find ourselves in situations analogous to John's, but we will face homiletical assignments in which logical, propositional language will be inadequate for the task. Time spent immersed in Revelation and other apocalyptic literature is therefore time well spent for rhetorical as well as theological reasons. Listen to the rhythmic flow of the language. See how the images emerge and fade, from the subtle to the phantasmagorical. Observe the beckoning landscapes where pain and suffering can be contained, truth and joy uncovered. Experience the movement of action and color as opposed to the drab and static nature of propositional language. And consider how the truth is painted rather than categorized. Sermons can work that way, too.

3. *Finding Our Own Images and Symbols*

Taking the form of the text seriously, then, means paying attention to the narrative movement, the symbolic language, and the evocative nature of the text, then asking what implications these may have for the sermon. One of the keys to preaching well from Revelation, since the book comes to us through images and symbols, lies, therefore, in finding those good meaning-bearing images and tensive symbols that will carry the freight of meaning one finds in John's work. In this section we consider three kinds of vessels for this task. Many of John's images came from the Hebrew scriptures. Some required work. John's images remain available to us. Some of them, too, will require work.

First, consider the sermon by Ron O'Grady in this collection. As a New Zealander, part of his heritage is that of being one of three million people in a country of seventy million sheep. He knows from experience that "if you are looking for a symbol of all that is weak and helpless, you would not find anything better than the tiny, woolly lamb."[14] From this natural image he moves to point out the utter irony of a slain lamb as savior of the world, the strength-in-weakness that characterizes the Christ-event and, for that matter, the whole Christian faith. His experience gives the sort of clarity to this unusual symbol from Revelation that few of us may have seen before. John, grounded in the Hebrew scriptures, reaches back to the Passover lamb for his imagery. For people not so firmly grounded as John, contemporary images like O'Grady's may serve to bring our hermeneutical horizon closer to that of the text.

When natural images like O'Grady's are not available, we may need to translate or contemporize John's pictures into symbols or narratives that will work for our people. Look, for example, at the picture in chapter 13, where the beast is loosed upon the earth to utter blasphemies against God for forty-two months. There seems to be little there for today's reader. But consider. For John this was the period prior to the end, the period in which they had to get ready for the last judgment. The blasphemous monster, identified with the Roman emperor, was a vivid image for Christians of John's day. For us, blasphemy has lost its impact. When an ayatollah condemns a writer to death for what are believed to be blasphemies against the prophet Mohammed, people cluck at the primitive nature of such action. Most of us have no place in our ethic where blasphemy is a serious problem and cannot identify with those, like John, who take it very seriously. We may need to stop and think again.

Once, on a cross-country trip, I stopped to eat at a roadside café. I was seated next to two of the most foul-mouthed persons I had ever encountered. Their vocabularies were utterly devoid of imagination and decency. Their lack of adjectives was itensified by the venom they injected into the few profane and obscene ones they possessed. Having lived and worked in oil fields, railroad crews, and lumber camps, I was used to all kinds of language. But under this unrelenting verbal barrage, my food and spirit finally lost their savor, and I gave up and left. Negative reinforcement works. I had had quite enough of that kind of language and longed for some Milton and Kazantzakis and John. And I could understand how those John is describing, satiated with blasphemy, could long for the Word of God. By extension, when we are satiated with the coarse things of this world, eating the tasteless bread of anxious toil (Psalm 127), spending ourselves for that which does not satisfy (Isaiah 55), and building bigger barns while our souls are in peril (Luke 12), we need to stop and listen for the gospel. Stories and images re-presented in modern settings may allow ancient truths to live again in the minds of people. While my two obscene characters are not the equivalent of a blasphemous Roman emperor of the first century, the debilitating effect of ungodly word-filth remains, as does the need for God's people to think on whatsoever things are true, honorable, just, pure, lovely, and gracious (Philippians 4).

This instance also calls to mind the truth that, for John and us, there must be *holy* before there can be *profane*. Blasphemy "works" parasitically off what is considered holy: God, heaven, salvation, love, sex, body, and so forth. If I had not had a deep-rooted sense of God's holiness, the "cussing" would not have affected me. This is why hearing people swear in a language not native to us is more droll than powerful. It lacks impact because we are not psychologically or spiritually vested in the "holy words" being profaned. For John, the power of evil is not self-actualized, but always a parody and perversion of the holy.[15]

The third possibility arises when we find ourselves in a situation where John's metaphor is no longer recognizable, but the original referent is still critically important. In chapter 8, following the opening of the seventh seal, a strange phenomenon appears: the star of Wormwood. It fell upon the waters and the waters were made bitter and the people died. In the previous chapter we saw the environmental overtones of this image, which are very powerful. There are also psychological overtones, which I once discovered when trying to preach on the text. In my study I discovered that people do not die from wormwood water. Wormwood is a bitter herb of the old world, but it is not lethal or even poisonous. We use the stuff in beverages! However, we can die of bitterness. So when John sees the star of Wormwood hurtling toward the earth as part of the woes that are to come before the final victory of God, perhaps he sees the danger of beleaguered Christians becoming bitter at their suffering and drowning in their bitterness. May God help us also to see that for the calamity that it was and is.

Consider also the bizarre scene in chapter 9 where the first woe commences with swarms of demon locusts. The locusts are commanded not to harm any green grass or any growth or any tree. They are to leave the earth alone. Their charge was to torture ungodly human beings. We still read occasionally of plagues of locusts, but not ones that act in such an abnormal way. We do, however, have other phenomena that function exactly like that, harming people while theoretically leaving the earth alone. Standing under this text, we can see the neutron bomb for the cruel instrument of torture that it would be. Further, lines that exclude, separate, or enslave, while invisible to the eye, wreak havoc with human lives and souls. One cannot see the Mason-Dixon line, but the separation for which it came to stand cost the United States some 620,000 lives. Words, too, are spoken and disappear in the ether. The earth does not remember; but people suffer and die because of them.

In these two examples, wormwood and demon locusts, entities alien to the contemporary hearer are translated into concepts that can be processed by them: bitterness and that-which-hurts-only-people. The point is not to be so one-dimensional as to say that John was predicting the neutron bomb. He was not. He was offering an image of nature itself gone awry in response to ungodliness. But the bomb and the other things mentioned function for us in the same way that the demon locusts functioned for him. And he can help us to see that if we will open our eyes to him and to the world around us.

We have considered three different ways to appropriate the imagery John uses: (1) natural correspondence (lamb to lamb), where John's image reaches all the way to our time with no loss of significance; (2) re-presentation (blasphemy to gutter language), where the strange Revelation scene is translated or contemporized into a scene more readily accessible to today's hearers; and (3) reconceptualization (wormwood to bitterness and demon locusts to that-which-hurts-only-people), where the referent of a no longer helpful metaphor is still vital.

4. *Trusting the Metaphor*

One last word on form is called for. I suggest that a distinction be made between the imagery in a Revelation-based sermon and the traditional sermon illustration. When we look for sermon illustrations, what we are normally looking for is something that will clarify or vivify some "point" that we are making, a story or image that will give life to the theological proposition that we have offered. We know how this works and, for my purposes here, it makes little difference whether we move from the point (deductive) or *toward* the point (inductive)—the illustration still functions in service of the proposition.

There are, to be sure, theological propositions in the book of Revelation that can be illustrated. However, oftentimes in this book the symbol or narrative *is* the point. The story itself is the truth-bearer. This raises the interesting question of whether or not the natural or translated imagery of our sermons can stand on their own as they do in John's letter. It makes a difference whether we trust the governing metaphor, be it story or image, to do its work, or whether we feel we must translate it into propositional language: "Now, what this story means is...."

This is high-risk/high-gain territory. By doing what John did—flinging his images toward the churches of Asia Minor—we run the risk that some people will not "get the point," will not make the connections necessary for the images to function in their lives. The gain is that for those who do, the impact is considerably more powerful because they have done the work of translation and application themselves. In this vein, scholars often say that while apocalyptic literature is difficult for us to understand, first-century readers would have been familiar and comfortable with the genre. I have some doubts about that, but I do believe that those who have struggled with the images and symbols, both then and now, are rewarded.

The wicket gate and the sea of glass are examples of images and stories that could carry the theological freight of a sermon. Ronald Allen's "With Eyes of Fire" is a vivid example, in this collection, of a governing metaphor allowed to do its work. G. B. Caird has said of Revelation that "much of the New Testament is written for those who have ears to hear, but this book is written for those who have eyes to see."[16] Allen does not neglect the ears, for his sermon takes seriously the poetic nature of apocalyptic, takes seriously the evocative nature of rhythm and repetition. But, within the framework of that rhythm, Allen repeatedly says, "I want you to see...." And we do see: scenes from Patmos so that we can look upon the cosmic Christ in all his power, with eyes of flaming fire; and then a variety of contemporary scenes in which struggling, suffering servants of that Christ are found in spite of everything to have that same fire in their eyes. Allen could have stated the theme propositionally—the power of Christ is greater than the strength of this world's principalities and powers—and then illustrated that point with a few appropriate anecdotes. But casting the message in terms of the image out of which it was born jerks our lazy eyelids up and demands that we...*see the fire*.[17]

It makes more sense, I think, to prepare our people in advance for what is coming and then, when it does, to trust them to do their Christian work, than it does to spoonfeed them propositions that will be forgotten by the time they hit the parking lot. When you find a vivid, compelling, "Christo-feric" story or image, resist the temptation to explain it to death. Do what John did. Send it forth.

Function

How do Revelation and Revelation-based sermons function for the communities that receive these words? Most recent Revelation studies tend to focus on two parallel and often overlapping concerns: the social and the literary function of the text. Let us consider these concerns with an eye toward the preaching ministry of the church.

1. Social Function

No serious student of Revelation will fail to note the difficult social and political circumstance in which the book was written and read. We must be careful here. Written by a Christian prophet to give hope, encouragement, and comfort to a marginalized and persecuted people, the book and its message may be trivialized when preachers use it to give hope and comfort to those who feel oppressed because they cannot buy a new Mercedes this year. Some homileticians have even suggested to me that Revelation is not a book for white middle-class North America: these people should not see themselves as the oppressed and will not see themselves as the oppressors.

Revelation as protest literature comes alive in the work and preaching of people like Allan Boesak and Marie Fortune. Boesak, struggling in South Africa against an oppressive government and its system of apartheid, writes that for the black people of South Africa, subject to persecution, banning, jail, torture, and murder,

"The Apocalypse is an exciting, inspiring and marvellous [sic] book."[18] The people read the book and can, in a very real sense, see it as addressed to them. His sermon here, preached before the recent hopeful stirrings in South Africa, is a marvelous example of God's ultimate power being proclaimed over against an oppressive government, and may be closer to the original ethos of Revelation than any other sermon here offered. Marie Fortune, whose sermon will doubtless prove to be the most controversial in this volume, spends her life in the struggle against sexual and domestic violence. Some people see the woman and child fleeing the dragon in Revelation 12 as no more than a folktale. But Fortune works every day with women and children fleeing from the wrath of brutal monsters. So, for Boesak and Fortune and other advocates for victimized people, where apocalypticism is not just a literary genre but a form of social ideology, the book functions exactly as John intended for it to function for those to whom he wrote.

How about the rest of us? I do not live in a community that generally functions under an apocalyptic ideology. In fact, when public figures like a Secretary of the Interior suggest that there is little reason to preserve the environment because the world is coming to an end soon, people tend to be greatly disturbed. But I do feel that we may be one major catastrophe away from a widespread resurgence of apocalypticism. A look at John's "system" may therefore be instructive. As Boring points out, "John sees Christian commitment in either/or, black/white, in/out terms in which there are no nuances."[19] He goes on to suggest that, for the contemporary reader, such an absolute stance is very difficult and our response—to the state, for example—is of necessity more nuanced.

This is correct. But I think we best not stray too far in these dangerous times from the judgment and hope that apocalypticism offers. At this point in time I stand under the judgment of John's apocalypticism, with my mostly sunny faith undergirding a mostly abundant life. But that could change. I think of the feelings that I had when I read John Calvin Batchelor's *The Birth of the People's Republic of Antarctica*, a dark theo-philosophical novel set in a crumbling world civilization of the late 1990s, and when I watched *The Day After* on television and saw Kansas City disappear in a mushroom cloud. I wondered: would we be able, in such settings, to offer our people the kind of hope that John offered to his people in their time of desperate need?

Although it is not a sermon, William Stringfellow's *An Ethic for Christians and Other Aliens in a Strange Land* is pertinent to our concern here. This Revelation-based book, written in 1973, had a powerful impact at the time. Stringfellow's point of departure was that there is great rejoicing in heaven when Babylon falls (19:1). As Babylon was for John a symbol of Rome, Stringfellow sees Babylon as a parable for America. (Note: Stringfellow does not assert that John wrote of Babylon with America in mind, but that for us Babylon functions as a parable for America.) In the cases of both Rome and America, according to Stringfellow, Babylon represents "the demonic in triumph in a nation."[20]

Stringfellow argues persuasively that the principalities and powers, including America, are wrapped up in what he calls a "death idolatry," and he issues a call—not just theological, but social—for people to resist the rule and power of death by saying "no" to death and "yes" to life:

> It is a person's involvement in that crisis in itself—whatever the apparent outcome—which is the definitively humanizing experience. Engagement in specific and incessant struggle against death's rule renders us human. Resistance to death is the only way to live humanly in the midst of the Fall.[21]

There is little of nuance in Stringfellow. We are on the side of death or of life. Choose this day.

We must remember that, from beginning to end, the author of Revelation claims to be a prophet delivering prophecy (see, e.g., 1:3; 22:9). Prophecy has less to do with predicting the future than it does with the claim that the message has been received through divine revelation and is delivered in the name and by the authority of God. Walter Bruggemann suggests that the purpose of prophetic ministry is to evoke an alternative consciousness to that of the dominant culture and that it does this by criticizing the culture and energizing the faith community.[22] John's work is in this tradition. And I think of those occasions when, uncomfortable as it may be, the contemporary preacher has no choice but to take the prophetic mantle upon him- or herself and proclaim the divinely given word of judgment and hope before a recalcitrant people. Revelation may or may not give us our text when that time comes. But we can take heart in the example of John, our brother, who shares with us in Jesus the tribulation and the kingdom and the patient endurance (1:9).

2. Literary Function

The literary function of an apocalyptic text is integrally related to form and content in what John Collins calls "the apocalyptic technique." This technique works to enable hearers to perceive a situation imaginatively and thus lay the basis for a creative, faithful course of action beyond what the raw facts of the situation might suggest.[23] It does this work by means of the images and symbols we have discussed, all seen under the aegis of God, who is both ultimately in charge and the revealer of how things are going to be.

Revelation's images are very powerful but also antiquated and, as we have seen, they sometimes need to be reconceptualized or replaced. But there is a deeper problem. Revelation was written as a support document for people up against what was perceived to be monstrous evil. Much of the imagery in the book is given over to visions of that evil at work. How are we to visualize the evil that threatens us? For people like Boesak and Fortune, the contemporary correspondences are clear. For others of us, they may not be so clear. And, as David Buttrick warns us, we must not image ourselves into absurdity.[24]

Take, for example, the slavering beast, a very evocative symbol. John's beast is grounded in that archetypal understanding of evil that calls up fearsome, bestial images. John looked to early Semitic examples like Tiamat and Leviathan. Modern examples like the great white shark in *Jaws* evoke the same feelings in us, as do others. I remember walking up to the pit at a rattlesnake round-up. The air was singing, the mass in the pit was seething, the hair on my neck stood up, and I was overwhelmed by a sense of malevolence and fear.

But think about it. Sharks, rattlesnakes and other beasts are not evil. In this setting they are but symbols that work at a preconscious level to generate a conscious activity, that of the imagination. According to Paul Wilson, "the spark of imagination happens when two ideas that seem to have no apparent connection are brought together."[25] And this is the key to the function of this image in the text. John places the beast, which has no basis in reality but which evokes powerful feelings, up next to Rome, which is very real. In his narrative he skillfully moves them closer and closer together until the spark jumps in the minds of his readers and they experience the primeval image of evil connected to the oppressive rule of Rome.

Now, are there any connections that our imaginations can make? Is there any reality in suburban North America that manifests such bestial evil at work destroying the lives of people? One person suggested to me that the Holocaust was such a beast. True. But, for most North Americans, the Holocaust is an event of historical, not personal, significance. In this collection both Peter Vaught and Marie Fortune give vivid answers. The best one that I can give is that evil is real, that we are not immune to it, that we encounter it in many and varied ways.

Beyond that, I can tell you how it has come to me. My "mostly sunny faith" was recently jerked to attention and called to account. What we expected to be a routine biopsy on my wife turned out not so routine. And we have been spiraled into the maelstrom of cancer, surgery, and chemotherapy, with all the attending shock and fear. Two things have amazed me: the outpouring of love, support, and prayer offered to and for us by church, colleagues, friends, and even strangers; and how, unbidden and unwanted, the beast has manifested itself to me. Cancer is utterly malevolent, powerful but cowardly, insidious, and damnably stupid—in short, it has all the evil qualities of John's beast.[26] And I have learned that you cannot convert cancer cells, you must kill them, with the unfortunate side effect that many good cells are destroyed in the process.

I come to see how apocalyptic thought and imagery function. As I stand beside this rattlesnake pit, I see the text through newly opened eyes. It functions for me in ways that would not have been possible several months ago. I see the beast and in all its malignancy and evil. And yet I believe, as Boring says in the sermon in this collection, God is stronger than the beast and "everything is going to be all right."[27]

3. Liturgical Function

Before leaving the questions of the social and literary functions of Revelation and Revelation-based sermons, a word should be added about the closely related liturgical function. Revelation was most probably written as a pastoral letter, a letter that John intended, not unlike the Pauline correspondence, to be read aloud during worship, and it was written for the purpose of offering encouragement and hope to beleaguered Christians during difficult and dangerous times, times when it seemed as if the end were near. A functional approach to our use of Revelation needs therefore to be attentive to those times, liturgical or otherwise, when Revelation might be particularly helpful to a congregation. These might include the last Sunday of the year (How long has it been since I have heard a good sermon on that down, post-Christmas Sunday?) or other times of dislocation, like Good Friday or Holy Saturday. It is also an appropriate resource during any season of crisis, being crisis literature itself.

Because there is so much hymnic material in Revelation, the question of hymns as sermon texts arises. Amos Wilder has written, "Before the message there must be the vision, before the sermon the hymn, before the prose the poem."[28] Revelation represents the earlier stage of each pair: vision, hymn, and poem. And the hymn by Jaroslav Vajda that closes this book represents such a first-stage reading of Revelation. Preaching from hymn texts in Revelation, the Psalter, and other places in the Bible is a matter of vigorous discussion among homileticians. See Thomas Troeger's sermon in this collection for a splendid example of preaching from a hymn text.

Further, because of its original function, form, and content, Revelation is good meat for drama; various kinds of musical interpretation, including opera; readers' theater; and other oral quasi-homiletical functions of worship, besides the traditional sermon. Since there are numerous eucharistic references in Revelation, many parts of the text are appropriate for use at the table.

Content

We come finally to the question of the content of the book itself, realizing that much of what has already been said about form and function applies here as well, since content is not divorced, especially in apocalyptic texts, from the purpose of the text and the way the text comes to us. The medium sometimes is the message. But in this section we are concerned particularly with hermeneutics and theology. There are some powerful contemporary messages in Revelation, like the sovereignty of God and the transcendence of Christ. How do we preach them? On the one hand, some of the themes in Revelation come to us as pure proclamation and can be offered as such. Balmer Kelly suggests that 7:9–17 can be seen like that: pure, unalloyed gospel, appropriate for Eastertide, when the church does not so much analyze the good news as simply proclaim it.[29] The performative language variously present in Revelation can also simply be proclaimed, trusting that it will do what it says: bless, curse, forgive, and so forth.[30] Other moves, symbols, and images within the text must be translated, as already mentioned, so that they can be processed by the hearer. For those pericopes where interpretation is required, our hermeneutical presuppositions come into play. If Revelation-as-prediction is rejected, how are we to interpret the thought of this difficult book?

1. Interpretative Models

A look at the main currents of interpretation popular in this century can be instructive here. There is a model, still used in some quarters, where a dogmatic scheme from outside the text (a trinitarian understanding of God, for example) is imposed upon the text. Another approach uses the developmental model based upon historical progression, in which, for example, an early war god gradually becomes the loving parent known through Jesus Christ. Both models have strengths and many weaknesses. A contemporary alternative is one in which the focus is upon the dialectic or polar structures of the text.[31] Rather than seeking to "harmonize" the text, as was the wont during the nineteenth century, the dialectical tensions in the text are seen as part of the text's essence and gift. This model is especially helpful when we come to Revelation, where so many tensions exist in such close proximity. Looking at them honestly gives us a more lifelike view of the world than one in which all the dichotomies are gratuitously harmonized by some abstract scheme. It also honors the text by evoking active participation, by issuing the vivid call to decide, to take a stand.

Look at some of the tensions evident in Revelation. Perhaps the great apocalyptic question, according to Boring, is addressed on every page: how can the Messiah have come and the world is not changed?[32] Others also leap out from the text. The tensions between Babylon and Jerusalem, the seal of Christ and the mark of the beast, the harlot and the bride, universal salvation and judgment, the sovereignty of God and the suffering of the saints, the Lord of history and the crucified one, the Pantocrator and the slain lamb, they are all there. A good example of this is found in this volume. Charles Blaisdell and James Altenbaumer, working independently of each other—and faithfully with the text, produced sermons entitled respectively: "The View from the Streets" and "The View from the Mountaintop." Both views are there. Dealing with these tensions in our preaching is more faithful to both the text and our current situation than ignoring them, because they exist in both places. Some are either-or situations; some are both-and. Since the sermons in this collection are drawn from Revelation, and like begets like, careful readers will not find a group of homogeneous sermons. The tensions of the book appear in the sermons as well, and some do not stand side by side comfortably. Different perspectives on the text give rise to different images. Consider how Cornish Rogers and Eugene Boring see similar things ("all is well," and "everything is going to be all right") in different texts, and how Peter Vaught and

Marie Fortune see different things ("accept God's grace" and "help God's grace be distributed") in the same text. Finally, this means that it is not only a challenge to preach from Revelation, it is also a challenge to hear and engage such sermons.

Confronting Revelation's tensions homiletically offers good opportunities for the inductive approach advocated by Fred Craddock ("not this, but this" and "it's true, and yet") as well as the homiletical reversals described by Eugene Lowry: a poor, helpless, slain lamb is the Lord of creation.[33] The synchronic images in Revelation may call to mind images from our own experience. I think of the last line of the last poem written by dying poet Ted Rosenthal: "Keep moving people. How could I not be among you?"[34] There is a double tension there that haunts me. Are we to keep moving ourselves or keep moving others or both? Was he bewailing the fact that he would not be among us to share the ongoing joys of life or was he somehow affirming that he would indeed be with us? I am, of course, not sure, but I suspect that Rosenthal intended both meanings both times. Whatever the case, it is not so much the meaning as it is the tension between meanings that gives the line its power. In this same vein Eugene Boring recalls the scene at the end of the film *Places in the Heart* where all the characters, living and dead, reassemble in church to receive the Lord's Supper. Our lives do not break down into orderly little packages. The various components that make us who we are overlap, like John's pictures and themes, to create the whole picture. I am a son, husband, and father, among other things. I am completely each one, but no one describes all that I am. We exist in a world of sin and suffering and yet we are, at the same time, richly blessed by God. "In the same night that we betrayed him, Jesus took bread and broke it and gave it to us."[35] Revelation is a good place to look for the total picture, tensions and all: judgment and grace intertwined, the end collapsing into a new beginning.

2. Theology and Theodicy

The most serious problem we face in seeking to preach from Revelation may not be the bizarre imagery and symbolism, but rather the theology that undergirds them. Seven-headed monsters are one thing; a God who unleashes terrible calamity upon the world is quite another. Some have even questioned whether or not the book is Christian.[36] All of our rationales and caveats are in place: Revelation is written in expressive, confessional language, not propositional and objectifying; the book is grounded in history but is not history itself. Therefore, the bloodthirsty God of vengeance and wrath, who rains fire and torment upon evildoers, is to be taken seriously but not literally.[37]

All our rationales notwithstanding, the fact remains that when we come to the text as preachers, we certainly find imagery and may find theology alien to our own time and understanding. What shall we do when we come to texts like 14:14–20, where the Son of Man uses a sharp sickle to harvest the "grain" of earth, while an angel throws the "grapes" into a winepress that flows with human blood as high as a horse's bridle for some two hundred miles? There appear to be five options.

(1) We can turn the page, conceding that we find the text theologically unacceptable and unredeemable. Sometimes we may have no choice but to do that. Even so, I suggest that we not rip the text out of our Bibles and throw it away, but rather place it in that drawer of our minds an old preacher labeled "awaiting more light." Biblical texts have a way, given time, of coming to light in a helpful way.

(2) We can try to resolve the problem. The Gandhian principle that if one presses a negative far enough, one finds a positive, may be operative here. G. B. Caird suggests that John's object in this text is

> to persuade the prospective martyrs that the world-wide carnage, in which their lives will be forfeit, will not simply be the vindictive work of Babylon; it will also be the gracious work of the Son of Man, sending out his angels to reap a great harvest of souls,...to tell his friends that Christ...can transform even the shambles of martyrdom into a glorious harvest home.[38]

This is an important message even in a world where martyrdom may be the farthest thing from people's minds. I remember reading of a woman taken hostage by a bank robber and held with a gun to her head during a high-speed chase. Asked later if she had been terrified, she replied that she had been at first, but then realized that "ultimately he could not hurt me." After that realization, she was at peace. This is John's message, too. And it works.

(3) We can use the text as a mirror. Adela Yarbro Collins offers that Revelation works by releasing the tension aroused in crisis through the phenomenon of catharsis. The fear of Rome is projected onto a cosmic screen where the ultimate outcome—God's victory—is clear, thus venting the fear.[39] Collins goes on to suggest that instead of

rejecting the violent images, symbols, and narratives, "one can use them as an occasion to uncover one's own hostile, aggressive feelings."[40] Having brought these feelings out into the light for critical examination, one may find creative ways of dealing with them. At least, that is the hope. Once, when environmentalist John Muir was persuaded to go on a hunt, he discovered a blood lust within himself and it frightened him:

> We little know how much wildness there is in us. Only a few generations separate us from our grandfathers who were savage as wolves....In the excitement and savage exhilaration of the pursuit, I, who have never killed any mountain life, felt like a wolf chasing the flying flock. But all this ferocity soon passed away, and we were Christians again.[41]

What emotions are evoked in us when we read of destruction on Revelation's scale? Can we call them forth, let them go, give them to God, and be Christians again?

(4) We can re-vision. By reducing the glare and noise of the text so that it does not produce shock and rising defense mechanisms, we allow people to hear the base message of God's justice. Those of us much vested in a God of unconditional love need to hear from time to time that God is not mocked and that God is our eternal friend but not our pal. Our purpose here is not to domesticate the text, but to reduce the shock value, thus giving people a chance to hear the text on a muted level rather than not at all. To those who counter that shock is part of the function of the text, I can only indicate my belief that while shock may have some value in engendering the mirror effect just described, it is vastly overrated as a source for the religious impulse.

When John's image is unfathomable to the modern mind, we may also find ways to re-image the text in a lateral move, without reducing its overall impact. For example, David Barr has suggested that the central theme of the Apocalypse is the proper worship of God.[42] Seen in this light, the text from chapter 14, together with other texts like 3:20 and 19:17–21, has eucharistic overtones and can be preached as a reminder that we "take" the elements of the Lord's Supper in the sure knowledge that we also shall be "taken."

(5) Some of the violent, troublesome imagery in Revelation may actually force us, in Ronald Allen's words, to "preach against the text."[43] One way to do this is to stand our text up against other texts

in which we find the gospel of Christ more salient. Allen speaks of the natural catastrophes in 8:6–9:21 as the judgment of God in John's view, while our experience is that natural disaster falls indiscriminately upon the just and the unjust. Against the earlier view, not credible to us, John also offers the promise of a time when God will be with us, all of us, and suffering will come to an end. In several places in the text rivers run blood and in chapter 14 the blood flows as high as a horse's bridle. But in God's city, the river that runs by the throne is clear as crystal. Thanks be to God.

3. A Narrative Vignette

I close the chapter with my attempt to deal with another difficult text. Chapter 6:1–8 introduces the long recital of the bad times to come that takes up most of the book. The first vision is the one that gives us the terrifying "Four Horsemen of the Apocalypse." John Lurvey has said that "Revelation is a book that is often seen in pictures, but not heard in pulpits."[44] That is especially true here. I have seen pictures, films, books—all based on this text; but I had never seen a sermon on 6:1–8 until Amanda Burr's sermon came to us. It is no mystery why preachers avoid this text. The four traditional purveyors of "war, famine, pestilence, and death" not only appear devoid of the gospel, they also are sent forth by God and the Lamb themselves, or at least with their permission! John seems to be shipwrecked on the problem of theodicy. And we are at sea as well. John has a God who is absolutely in charge, which is no easy matter for us, especially after the Holocaust. And this is complicated by John's God authoring or permitting terrible evil. I offer this narrative vignette as a way of re-visioning the text if not resolving the problem. Readers must determine if the criteria of being faithful to the text, faithful to the gospel, and helpful to the understanding of late-twentieth-century people, are fulfilled.

Ride On?

The four men sat in the back corner of the skid row bar. The dim light from the neon beer signs cast soft shadows upon sinister faces. Of the four, one was massive, the other three slight. The large man, black and brooding, slowly raised his hands to his chin. His shirt sleeves fought a losing battle to contain the bulging muscles of scarred arms. He looked into the corner and said, "War."

"It's the easiest way," he continued, "because they like it. They will run *from* you," he gestured at the others, "but they run *toward* me." His dark face broke into a sardonic smile. "A little mistrust here, some bruised egos there, a little accident perhaps, and they will break out their weapons and martial music. Then the blood lust will take them and...selah!" he threw up his arms, "They will slaughter each other gladly. Beloved," he said, staring into the corner, "it is the best way."

"No," said the one to his left. "War is loud and messy and very expensive." The gaunt brown man's voice came in soft Spanish cadences. He was half the size of the black man, but faced him squarely. "Hunger is better. War energizes; hunger enervates. With war you get those who think they have won. With hunger, Beloved, you have hollowness and emptiness and then nothing. The hungry don't think in terms of righteous causes. They just suffer quietly and die."

"You have a point," said the Asian, as he lifted his thoughtful face. "But my way is better still. War and famine are selective. Leaders survive wars and the wealthy survive famine. But pestilence has no regard for border, cause, or social status. In the past I have wiped out more of them than both of you put together. Give me leave to set loose a good plague and watch the results. More widespread than hunger; more cost-effective than war. Choose my way, Beloved, and you will see."

You could call the fourth man white, although he was actually a pale and sickly-looking green. He had picked up the nickname "Antichrist" in his youth because he found the brass crosses on communion tables to be good tools for smashing into Coke machines in the churches he vandalized, but that was long before he had found his real calling. He had been silent during the meeting thus far. He looked in turn at the black, brown, and yellow faces of his comrades. "It does not matter," he said. "The point is death. They deserve to die and they will. Your methods are good. I am willing to see all of them put to use, plus any others," he smiled slightly, "that come to me in the heat of the moment. Use us all, Beloved," he said as he turned toward the corner. "Use us all and there will be no escape."

The four men sat silently, looking at the shadowed figure in the corner. Finally she sighed and leaned forward. God's lovely face was creased by an ineffable sadness. She began to speak. "Your calling me Beloved offends me. You represent the forces of history that threaten my world." God's eyes narrowed. "Your love is false and I am not deceived. You exist because of sin. If I destroy you, I destroy freedom and that I will not do. So I will use you. But there is something you should know."

God reached down and picked up her child, who had been sitting quietly on the blanket God had placed by her chair. "You see this child of mine," she said. "Henceforth forevermore, this child shall be your master. Do whatever you will to subvert my plan, and the child will inject into that madness a saving possibility. Wreak all your havoc and this child will find a way to keep my purpose and my promise at work. You will think you are winning and many of them will also think you are winning and will despair. But, mark my words, this little child will defeat you all."

"Ridiculous!" sneered Death. And the Four Horsemen began a staccatto litany, their voices dripping with venom: "Auschwitz, Hiroshima, My Lai, Chernobyl...; nuclear weapons, toxic waste, cancer, AIDS...; Star Wars, starvation, meaninglessness, sin...."

God raised her hand for silence. "In...my...good...time," she said, measuring her words, "This child will defeat you all. It is already written in my heart."

"The child better have plenty of friends, Beloved!" spat Death.

"The child has me," said God. "That is enough. Even so, you shall see how many friends we have. You shall see. Now go."

One by one they got up from the table: War, Famine, Pestilence, and Death. The baby boy watched intently as the four men departed, slipping away into the foggy darkness, there to bide their time. God scooped up the child and held him in her arms. She looked at the doorway. She looked at the child. She looked at the old "Miller High Life" sign over the bar, in which the word *Life* was buzzing and flickering, like it was about to go out.

She shook her head. She picked up the blanket and started to leave. "They shall see," was all she said.

Notes

[1] Ian Maclaren (John Watson), *Beside the Bonnie Briar Bush* (New York: Dodd, Mead & Co., 1895), pp. 26-31.

[2] See, for example, Adela Yarbro Collins, "Reading the Book of Revelation in the Twentieth Century," *Interpretation* 40 (July 1986): pp. 235-237.

[3] Austin Farrer, *The Revelation of St. John the Divine* (Oxford: Clarendon Press, 1964), p. 4.

[4] Eugene Lowry, "The Difference Between Story Preaching and Narrative Preaching," in *Papers of the Annual Meeting of the Academy of Homiletics* (1988): p. 141.

[5] John J. Collins, *The Apocalyptic Imagination* (New York: Crossroad, 1987), pp. 13-14.

⁶Daniel Berrigan, *Beside the Sea of Glass* (New York: Seabury Press, 1978), pp. 11-12.

⁷*Ibid.,* pp. 29, 31.

⁸Adela Yarbro Collins, "Reading the Book of Revelation," p. 239.

⁹*Pilgrim's Progress* is an allegory and not an apocalypse in the strictest sense of the term. Nevertheless, it has many elements in common with Revelation, not the least of which was its composition *in absentia,* prison vis-a-vis exile. Both works picture a new world over against this one, the eventual deliverance of the just, and a heavenly celebration on the arrival of the redeemed, among other things.

¹⁰John Bunyun, *Pilgrim's Progress,* cited in G. A. Studdert-Kennedy, *The Wicket Gate* (Garden City, N.Y.: Doubleday, Doran & Co., 1929), p. 11.

¹¹Peter Fribley, "Intervening Angels: Preaching and the Art of Rembrandt van Rijn," Lecture at the Annual Meeting of the Academy of Homiletics, Pittsburgh, Pa., 6 Dec 1986.

¹²M. Eugene Boring, Lecture given at Texas Christian University, Fort Worth, Tex., 18 Jan 1988.

¹³John M. Lurvey, Jr., "Reclaiming the Apocalypse for Preaching," unpublished manuscript, 23 Dec 1980, School of Theology at Claremont, Claremont, Calif., p. 2.

¹⁴See p. 85.

¹⁵The ideas in this paragraph emerged in a discussion with Eugene Boring.

¹⁶G. B. Caird, *The Revelation of St. John the Divine,* Harper's New Testament Commentaries (New York: Harper & Row, 1966), p. 13.

¹⁷See pp. 54, 61.

¹⁸Allan A. Boesak, *Comfort and Protest* (Philadelphia: The Westminster Press, 1987), pp. 37-38.

¹⁹Boring, "Introduction to Revelation," unpublished manuscript, 13 Dec 1987, Texas Christian University, Fort Worth, Tex., p. 89.

²⁰William Stringfellow, *An Ethic for Christians and Other Aliens in a Strange Land* (Waco, Tex.: Word Books, 1973), p. 33.

²¹*Ibid.,* p. 138.

²²Walter Bruggemann, *The Prophetic Imagination* (Philadelphia: Fortress Press, 1978), pp. 13-14.

²³John J. Collins, *The Apocalyptic Imagination,* p. 32.

²⁴David G. Buttrick, *Preaching Jesus Christ* (Philadelphia: Fortress Press, 1988), p. 66.

²⁵Paul Scott Wilson, *Imagination of the Heart* (Nashville: Abingdon Press, 1988), p. 34.

²⁶See Thomas G. Long's analysis of cancer as "beast" in "Preacher and the Beast: From Apocalyptic Text to Sermon," *Papers of the Annual Meeting of the Academy of Homiletics* (1988), pp. 87-88.

²⁷See pp. 75ff.

²⁸Amos Wilder, *Theopoetic* (Philadelphia: Fortress Press, 1976), p. 1.

²⁹Balmer H. Kelly, "Revelation 7:9–17," *Interpretation* 40 (July 1986), p. 294.

³⁰Long, "Preacher and the Beast," pp. 66-71.

³¹I am indebted to my colleague Toni Craven for many of the ideas in this paragraph.

³²Boring, Lecture given at Texas Christian University, Fort Worth, Tex., 1 Feb 1988.

[33]See Fred B. Craddock, *As One Without Authority*, Third Edition (Nashville: Abingdon Press, 1979) and Eugene Lowry, *The Homiletical Plot* (Atlanta: John Knox Press, 1980).

[34]Ted Rosenthal, *How Could I Not Be Among You?* (New York: George Braziller, 1973), p. 74.

[35]See Sanders, *God Has a Story, Too* , pp. 48-51.

[36]J. P. M. Sweet, *Revelation*, Westminster Pelican Commentaries (Philadelphia: Westminster Press, 1979), pp. 48-51.

[37]See Boring, *Revelation*, pp. 51-59 and 112-119.

[38]Caird, *The Revelation of St. John the Divine*, pp. 193-194.

[39]Adela Yarbro Collins, *Crisis and Catharsis: The Power of the Apocalypse* (Philadelphia: The Westminster Press, 1984), p. 153.

[40]*Ibid.*, p. 173.

[41]John Muir, *John of the Mountains, The Unpublished Journals of John Muir*, Linnie Marsh Wolfe, ed. (Madison, Wis.: Univ. of Wisconsin Press, 1979), p. 199.

[42]David Barr, "The Apocalypse of John as Oral Enactment," *Interpretation* 40 (July 1986), p. 255.

[43]See Ronald J. Allen, "Preaching Against the Text," *Encounter* 48 (Winter, 1987), pp. 105-115.

[44]Lurvey, "Reclaiming the Apocalypse for Preaching," p. 1.

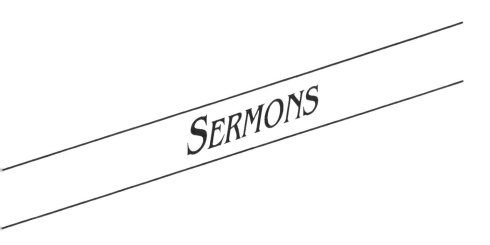

SERMONS

Prelude

PREACHING ON THE EVE OF A NEW MILLENNIUM

James A. Forbes, Jr.

In less than a decade a most significant event will take place. December 31, 1999, will move toward the waning moments of the year. In the final seconds digital clocks will advance from 1-9-9-9 to 2-0-0-0. The beginning of a new millennium.[1] Can you imagine what that New Year's celebration will be like? Think of the weeks and months and years as that magic moment approaches. When 1-9-9-9 becomes 2-0-0-0, Times Square will not be able to hold all of us. In fact, there will be no need, because all over the world, before the stroke of twelve, arrangements will have been made for welcoming the New Age. I suspect that expeditions will have arrived at the closest point to the International Date Line so that persons can claim to be the first ones to welcome the new millennium. In the name of one-upmanship some firm will probably have contracted for an outer-space voyage to be a greeting party for the brand new day. You will be able to see the fireworks even from distant vantage points. I cannot think of any person of reasonable health and aware-ness, as the day draws near, who will be indifferent to this once in a ten-lifetime opportunity.

In the religious community there is special concern. Particularly those of us who read from Genesis to Revelation have already been

James C. Forbes is senior minister of The Riverside Church in New York City. "Preaching on the Eve of a New Millennium" is adapted from his inaugural address as Joe R. Engle Professor of Preaching at Union Theological Seminary, New York. We express appreciation to the Union Seminary Quarterly Review, where the address first appeared in print in 1988.

impressed by the reality of a certain time span—one thousand years. In the light of eschatological consideration it may be very heavy for us to bear or too light to give consideration. For example, in J. B. Phillips' translation of Revelation he speaks of weighty symbols, including the year 1000 or a thousand-year period. He says the images in the Book of Revelation—the crowns, the thrones, the gold, the jewels, the colors, the trumpet, the violence of actions, and the impact of incredible numbers and awe-inspiring sights— are all images that stir that threshold of the brain where monsters lurk and supernatural glories blaze. John in these images is stirring, with a kind of surrealistic artistry, the vastness of our unconscious minds. Now, I assume that some would say it has not touched them quite so deeply. Perhaps the sentiments in this audience might be much more reflected in the response of John Calvin to the issue of the millennia. He said of the millennians, who limited the reign of Christ to 1000 years, "Their fiction is too puerile to deserve refutation." So it is clear that not everybody is equally excited about 1000 years. But I suspect that will be changing.

I contend that as the year 2000 draws near we had better know something about millennial language. We wouldn't want our students to be like the student being examined by an ordination board who was asked, "What is your position with respect to the various millennial positions?" And he said, "Which ones?" The answer was, "Well, tell us, are you premillennialist, postmillennialist or amillennialist?" After a pregnant pause the student said, "I'm a panmillennialist." "Now what does that mean?" "It means I believe that everything is going to pan out all right," he replied.

Let me hasten to make it clear that it is not my intention to reintroduce apocalyptic language nor to debate the merits of a particular school of eschatological thought. What I intend to share is my strong impression that the year 2000 is a powerful moment that has already begun to beckon and will increasingly place before us an invitation—one we will find it difficult to ignore. It will become a siren call luring us to both its promise and its perils. The prospect of attending Celebration 2000 will occasion fresh visions, will spark utopian impulses, will provoke cosmic critique, will stimulate goal-setting and a quest for new ways and new means. Ultimate questions will be raised about the meaning of human history and where God fits in, what matters and why, who belongs, how to survive, who is for us, who is against us, and what are the limits—can they be broken or are they guaranteed? As that year approaches there will be dreams and new schemes and surely disappointments and dashed hopes. We will experience conspiracies and maybe tyrannies, breakthroughs, and breakdowns. I am convinced that that year, whether one is premillennialist, postmillennialist, amillennialist, or panmillennialist, is bound to touch a deep place in every heart.

We will get a chance to look at history from the perspective of this unique moment as well as to think in terms of a thousand years. In other words, those of us who have gently allowed ourselves to sing hymns that speak of "a thousand ages in thy sight are like an evening gone, short as the watch that ends the night, before the rising sun," will discover that that word *thousand* is more serious than we had imagined.

Most people do their best to make life what it ought to be. But when their energy has been expended, they become aware that some things will not happen until the right time comes. Therefore, people of faith and destiny live their life with significant lusting after *kairos*. Most of life's promises are realized on clock time— *chronos*. But if we could ever find the time that implies the breaking forth beyond clock time, the pregnant moment of divine possibility, then things would begin to fall into place. There would be a time of peace, of prosperity, of completeness, of fulfillment. I suspect that many of you, like myself, have spent time waiting for *kairos*— looking for a change of season, waiting for our next birthday, looking forward to a special national holiday, a religious holy day, an anniversary, school opening or closing, or some new state of life. We keep looking. But who on earth will be able to resist the prospect, as the year 2000 rolls around, that we will be able to see *chronos* come to a moment of pregnant pause. I believe this is going to happen. Given the way *chronos* moves we are already on the eve of that kind of moment. A moment that will allow us to be fully human. A moment in which we keep an eye open for divine possibilities never before imagined.

Having made this claim, what does that have to do with preaching? Preaching is always related to the persistent prevailing problematic moods and trends of any age. We do not yet know all the possibilities. People with the skill to activate the dialogue between God and the contemporary scene have been given the power of inspiration, transformation, and healing. They have been given a nourishing spirit for faith education and have cultivated the talent for the facilitation of that celebration. Parishioners who have heard the call to Celebration 2000 will turn to sensitive and informed preachers who shed light on the issues affecting our ability to answer the invitation.

Of course, the pulpit is not the center from which *all* wisdom will flow. Congregations will also be able to sense what is happening and to understand the forces at work—megatrends as well as minitrends. People will not look to the pulpit as the only channel of insight about what is going on in the world. There are people in secular pursuits who are also people of faith who will be visited by the angel of truth and will be given insight. Unless the people in the pulpit and those who are preparing to stand in the pulpit take time to hear those in the pews, we may have deficient analysis and may actually miss out on who will make it to Celebration 2000. And we must make our reservations now. RSVP, if you will. What are the conditions in the world, as you see them, between now and 2000 that will determine whether we reach that point at all? Will we reach it with joy and great anticipation? I put R-S-V-P on my paper and I jotted down what these mean to me. How about you? What strikes you as critical in living toward the new millennium that is being prepared for us?

✳ ✳ ✳

Whatever you think, I hope it has some space for the consideration of what we will do in the area of RESOURCES—natural as well as human resources. There are those who are saying whether we get there may be largely determined by the degree of wisdom with respect to the stewardship of our resources. What will we do? Will we be able to learn to conserve? Will we learn how to come to a more equitable distribution of these resources? Will we find a way to gain access to resources without hastening the day of the exhaustion of the planetary energy reserves? What we do about resources will make a list of differences to what Celebration 2000 is going to look like. Preachers will have to have a role in helping us deal with our resources. I am very concerned.

We worry about material and human resources, but what are we going to do in the area of the SPIRITUAL foundations for human existence? We live in a secular age. We live in a time when the old spiritual verities are no longer immediately available to us. Louis Dupre describes this spirituality in a secular age by saying that some few sectors of the population are experiencing the reality of the transcendent in the same way as their forebears while others are manufacturing a kind of reasonable facsimile of that original experience. Most of us do not feel, do not experience the presence of the transcendent in the ways of our forebears. Even our youthful experience of awe and wonder at the face of God no longer carries that aura of the *mysterium tremendum*. Part of being the ones who may survive to the year 2000 means that much of what we knew for sure about the reality of God can no longer be affirmed with the same kind of wide-eyed wonder we once knew. What shall we do? Shall we reach back for the same old way? Shall we persist in saying if God is not here in the same way, then there is no God? Shall we allow God to advance to the year 2000—as if we could do anything to prevent it? Are there new ways? Are there new patterns? Are there new dynamics that are eternal without causing us to abandon the responsibility for our time?

Then there is the issue of VALUES. How we get into the world, what means we will use, in what context we will develop, what relationships will be like once we are here, the patterns of life in terms of the rituals by which we enter into community, what means we discern when it is time to terminate certain patterns in community whether they are personal, social, or international in scope, are all issues being raised. Even the ethicists acknowledge that they are not able to keep up with all the choices we make or which way we go on the primary issues of life and death. We are called upon, as we move to the year 2000, to find the wisdom to look at old problems to find what it is from the past that still works and what it is that has not yet been tried that may be a gift to us in our time. Serious attention must be given to clarification and transformation of values.

Besides the issues of resources, spiritual development, and value shifts from all levels, we must recognize that we have to do all this work in an increasingly PLURALISTIC environment. Groups of people with differing faith claims, different vested interests, different perspectives on life are all vying for the role of director of our future. There you have it. RSVP. Will we make it? Will we make it in joy? Will we make it intact? Will pluralistic complications push us over the edge with respect to peace? Can we have peace in a pluralistic arrangement where there are limited resources and there is the possibility of losing the foundations of our spiritual mores as our values come unglued? Can we make it? Will you be there? Can I count on your presence? I have lifted these issues, along with the ones in your thoughts, in order to say something about the kind of preaching that is going to be necessary.

As people all over the world begin to look forward to the year 2000 and consider the multiple RSVP complications that will determine whether we're going to make it or not, preaching for this new age will have to presuppose diversity of perspective. Preachers cannot get away with assuming that they have the only track to truth or that their style is the only style, or their approach the only approach. We must find somewhere in the world that can train preachers who can deal with the multiplicity of our hopes and aspirations. Preachers must know how to hear the cries in various communities, understand different language patterns, and know how to communicate through different media. People who are capable of hearing the question and then using the critical development of their resources will be able to join in the process of correlation. In these times of vanishing unanimities preachers will have to be able to hear, then to speak; then having spoken, they need to hear what is spoken back to what has been said and learn how to incorporate the data they gather and keep on keeping on. In this day, preachers who never get down to the cause of the problem are out.

Preaching will have to be biblically grounded. Preachers will have to know the scriptural traditions from Genesis all the way to the gory details of Revelation. They must know the tradition and know where in the tradition to connect with the multiplicity of problems we face.

They must have biblical and theological depth as well as a kind of historical grasp. You do not get to the year 2000 and wait for *kairos* without taking seriously the *kairotic* elements involved in the *chronos*. They have got to know history. They must find a way to deal with times of oppression and times of darkness. When it is dark, they must know how to mount a visual, dramatic display where the darkness does not obscure the possibility of the new dawn.

They must get folks ready even before they know they are ready. They must teach even when people do not want to hear, even when they are not interested. Many times the question emerges too late and we try to provide a framework of meaningful interpretation of history and life. When that happens, it is too late. We must prepare in advance of their asking the questions about Celebration 2000 and RSVP some prevenient, preoperative instruction, getting them ready for the day to come. There must also be a kind of patience not to be impressive. A patience to turn people toward reality. A patience to lead them to sacrifice. A patience to lead them to risk alternative approaches to fulfillment. A patience to help them learn rejoicing on the way, even before the full cause of rejoicing has been revealed. They must know how to address the deep places. They must know how to tap into the stored treasures of existence so that there will not only be enlightenment bantering back and forth, but getting into the deep unconscious, nonconscious dimensions of our existence. From there the new possibilities will emerge.

They must know more than just how to give good delivery. They must be agents with power to bring deliverance. That is, a sermon is not finished when we say, "Amen." The sermon is finished when our *Amen* has taken up active, transformative possibilities in a social, economic, and political context.

Preaching for this day must involve gifts of criticality, as well as a capacity for conservation and innovation. Partnering with people is crucial. They need to know that you are with them as they seek to face that great celebration.

We must understand that tapping into the deep life experiences of people can not all be done from the pulpit. There has to be a liturgical framework. Renewed preaching alone will not do. Liturgical reform is absolutely necessary for the year 2000.

We must understand not only liturgical reform but the arts, music, dance, drama, and the whole process of the depth of human response. Preachers who somehow separate themselves, belittle those dimensions, or think of them as preliminary or background will not be ready for the day.

Then there is embodiment. You have to be something when you move toward 2000. It is not enough to say something, you have to *be* something.

In closing, I have work to do. I have received the invitation to the year 2000. I bring that invitation to you and call upon you, brothers and sisters, to be willing to receive the invitation. There is a celebration planned and you are all invited. If you are unable to come, send proxies; a new generation, a new body, a new consciousness, a new world. I do not know what you are going to do. Some of you may feel you are too old to make it. Do not despair. In the book of Isaiah a man called Hezekiah was told by a messenger sent from the Lord, "You can't make it." Hezekiah prayed and again the messenger appeared, this time with good news. In God's mercy Hezekiah was granted an additional fifteen years.

Certainly none of us can boast of certainty but we must live with hope and trust that we will be there. I have made my request to the Lord. I am going to be there and I have every confidence that I will make it. But wait a minute. Let me explain what I mean. If you look for me at Times Square, I may not be there. It could be too crowded. If you go to the International Date Line and watch for me, I may not be there. I may not be able to afford to get there. If you look for me in outer space somewhere, I may not be there. I am not going to guarantee where I will be. But if you do not find me in Times Square, come on up to a city built foursquare. I will be there! I hope you will be there! I am looking for you. Meet me. Meet me for Celebration 2000.

Note

[1]Ed. note: We are aware of the argument that, technically, the twenty-first century does not begin until 2001, since there was no year numbered "0." Nevertheless, most people will celebrate the new century and millennium on January 1, 2000, and Dr. Forbes' call to "get ready" is no less urgent, whatever calendar one uses.

THE VIEW FROM THE STREETS

Charles R. Blaisdell

John's vision, there at the beginning of the book of Revelation, is almost too much for words. But words must somehow suffice—they must somehow make do to convey the stunning clarity, the majesty, and the power of what John has seen. He had to *try* to put it into language, even if language was not fully adequate to the task. "I saw," says John, "seven golden lampstands," and, in their midst, "one like the Son of Man," enfolded in a golden girdle, with flaming feet and hair—and holding the very stars themselves in his hands! Stunning! Incredible! Language strained to its very limits—and maybe beyond them.

That is what poetry is—and poetry is what language must try to become when we seek to describe the truly sublime, the truly glorious. A few years ago, I flew to New York City to spend the Thanksgiving holiday with some friends. And the weekend began in a glorious way. For, as I was riding there high in the air, suddenly the plane poked its nose through the clouds and streaming into my window came the sight of Manhattan in all its beauty and glory. There, on the left, close enough to touch it would seem, were the twin towers of the World Trade Center, lit up by the reflected sun like two golden torches. And there below me was the Statue of Liberty, then encased in scaffolding for repairs like a cuddling cocoon made out of match sticks. Up to the north was the Empire State

---

Charles R. Blaisdell is associate regional minister of the Christian Church (Disciples of Christ) in Indiana.

Building, the very center of the city, majestically poking its head toward the clouds, and yet almost delicate-looking, bathed that day in a blue and orange light. And then as the plane banked into a stomach-tickling roll, there below me was the Verrazano-Narrows Bridge, whose spiderlike cables and towers stood in amazing contrast to the deep blue-green of the Atlantic Ocean spreading infinitely to the horizon so very far away. It was indeed a scene to take your breath away, a scene that cried out for poetry to describe it.

And surely, I thought, in this moment of awe and wonder, surely God is here and is to be praised for such beauty. And just as surely John also knew that God was to be praised for the beauty of *his* vision, the God who stood there among those lampstands, the one whose glory words could only grope to depict.

Yet, as airplanes will, my plane began to descend, making a sweeping arc over Staten Island and heading over Brooklyn toward the airport. But as we descended, the stunning majesty and beauty and glory of that vision of the skyline was slowly replaced—the view from 5000 feet became the view from 500, 100, 50 feet, and finally the view from street level. And the aerial view had been replaced—replaced by scenes of the burned-out tenements, and the graffiti-covered commuter trains, and the junkyards of abandoned cars, and the winos huddling over the steam grates for a little Thanksgiving warmth.

What had become of the beauty of that aerial vision? Where now was the glory that had been so apparent before? Where were those lampstands and the one who stood among them like a Son of man?

Where was God now? What was God doing? The aerial view of things had come so easily and clearly; the view from the streets was so much more difficult, so much more full of pain and ambiguity. What could it mean from this perspective, from street level, to say that "God is the Alpha and the Omega," the one who, in the words of one Bible scholar, is "the sovereign Lord of all times and all ages...the beginning and the end of history, and the Lord of all that lies between"? What does that mean, there at street level?

And John's own question, as he wrote the book of Revelation, the question that lies behind his vision, is not so different from our question—yet with one terrifying difference. For those to whom John wrote were persecuted, facing actual torture and death simply for being Christians. The year was about 95 A.D., and Roman power had never seemed mightier. A generation earlier, Roman armies had burned the temple (and Jerusalem with it), and now Rome was systematically carrying out a policy of exterminating Christians. In such a situation, who wouldn't be afraid? Who wouldn't be tempted to believe that the bets had been placed on the wrong horse, a horse who seemed now to be running far back of the pack? Who wouldn't fear death—both the hideousness of it and the seeming futility of it? Who wouldn't be tempted to believe that there was a power at work in the world at odds with God—and maybe even greater than God!—which inevitably crushed and maimed life and hope?

And while you and I need not fear for our *lives* simply for counting ourselves as Christians, who among us—you or I—has not experienced the same chilling question of whether God may just not be as powerful as those demonic forces in the world that starve children, that make nuclear bombs, that cause us to think that the good is slowly being crushed out of life, leaving, like the grape in the wine press, only the hulls and husks of what we had hoped might be? Who has the power!? That's the question. *Is* there really *any* power over hopelessness, meaninglessness, death, and madness? Or is it only from the aerial view of things, the view from 5000 feet, removed from where people really live, that we can see "one like the Son of Man"—but not from the streets below?

It's a question we cannot ignore. Especially now, especially as another Thanksgiving begins the way to another Christmas. For who among us has not sometimes felt a certain letdown as the season has wound its way down? Which one of us has not sighed a little as the brightness and the promises of Advent have dulled into Christmas afternoon? Who among us has not wondered whether the glad tidings, the warmth and the smells and the feastings must give way to what we might call a more "realistic" appraisal of things? "Come, ye thankful people, come"—why? "Peace on earth, good will to all…."—so what? "A multitude of the heavenly hosts"— so what? What does all of this really have to do with the world in which we really live, what does it have to do with the world at street level? Haven't *you* ever wondered in the small hours of the night?

And here, the word that God speaks to John might just seem to be one more bit of religious naiveté: "Do not be afraid…says the Lord God,…[for] I am…[the one] who is and who was and who is to come" (1:8, 17, interlaced). In fact, it's not just naive, it's downright crazy-sounding. For what person in his or her right mind wouldn't fear—at least sometimes? What person wouldn't despair—at least sometimes. What person wouldn't at least wonder sometimes, in the face of the world viewed from street-level, in the face of the world where you and I really live?

But, in passing this vision on to us, John is *not* being naive, he is *not* just living life from the aerial view, he's *not* just preaching pie in the sky by and by. For John's message to us is this: yes, the powers of death and despair live, but God has promised that they shall not have the final word. Indeed, God's creation sometimes groans, but behind that groaning can be heard the sounds of God battling with us with the weapons of invincible love to bring all creation to its appointed end. God can be trusted, come what may. That's the simple good news that John's revelation confronts us with. And to believe this is to know that God is not just some far-off future power, but is the one who "is to come," who is to come even now. And to know this is to know that our efforts to fight despair and hopelessness in the here and now are not futile, do not go for nothing, for God fights there with us, God offers to us the strength and the comfort to carry on, God works with us always and forever in the hopes of making our lives the best they can be.

God can be trusted. That is the message of John's vision. That is the message of the gospel. But what does that mean? What *does* God do? You and I have lived too much to believe that God makes everything all right, that God gives us whatever we want, that God spares us from all pain, all mixed feelings, all loss. We have lived too much to believe that. The God we worship is neither a magician nor a cosmic air traffic controller, keeping everything on an even path.

But God can be trusted to be God—and what that means on this Thanksgiving is the same as it has always meant. It means that God offers to each and every one of us in each and every moment the possibility of richer lives. It means that God offers the vision of the good to us when all we thought possible was despair. It means, as the prophet Isaiah also discovered, that God can offer to us the notion of running when walking was all we thought was possible. It means that when we want to collapse in the dust that threatens to envelop us, God offers to us a way to walk onward. It means that we can be shown ways even to take to life with "wings like eagles" where we had thought that we must be forever pedestrians, trapped in pedestrian lives.

And so I got off that plane at La Guardia Airport, and I took a cab to my friends' house, where seven of us, old friends from high school and college, celebrated Thanksgiving. At the meal we asked my friend Bob to say grace. Now I must warn you that Bob's prayers can be rather, shall we way, eccentric, and yet always to the point. And this prayer was no exception, for Bob bowed his head and offered the following by way of saying grace: "I look around this table," Bob said, "and I think of similar gatherings in the past, and what has happened to each of us over the years. I see separations, divorce, new jobs, bitter leave-takings, a marriage ended by death, lives turned upside down. And yet," he continued, "my prayer is this: I raise my glass to toast us and to toast God—for like the country ham that we have tried to overcook today and yet which has surprised us with its resiliency and with its ability to taste good no matter what we have inflicted on it, we too, with God's help, have not only endured but we have prevailed. We have been brought back together again in hope and in power and in new life by the one whose power shall never fail us."

And Bob said, "Amen," and I said, "Amen," and we all said, "Amen." For Bob was right on that Thanksgiving Day—for each of us *had* seen, just as John had seen, just as each one of you has seen, God standing there in the middle of our lives, standing there among *our* lampstands, keeping those lamps from burning out—and kindling them, in fact, to burn even more brightly in the rich air of new beginnings, fueled with the vision that life can be lived beautifully. And not just from the aerial view, but even from street level.

Prayer: "Gracious God and good, you do stand in our midst, you do uphold and guide us, you do nurture and comfort us. For all your blessings indeed we give you thanks, for the love that will not let us go, we are indeed grateful. Amen."

WITH EYES OF FIRE

Ronald J. Allen

I want you to see the sun,
    white-hot
        hanging in the sky
            over the ocean.

        Not a breath of air is stirring.
        110°
        White hot.

On a tiny island,
    rocky and volcanic,
        a Roman ship has landed,
            and a small group is herded off
                at sword-point
                and is left,
                      sweltering in the humidity.

        The only sound the lonesome gull.
        The only movement the buzzing of a fly.
        The only color the fierce blue of the sea.

Ronald J. Allen is associate professor of preaching and New Testament at Christian Theological Seminary, Indianapolis, Indiana.

Patmos.
Where someone named John wrote the book of Revelation.
Patmos.
No wonder he had visions there.

Patmos and the little islands like it
    functioned as low-budget political prisons
        where Caesar could trash those
           who were a threat
                to his brand of law and order.

A little group meets on Patmos,
    in the backroom of a house on a back street,
        gathered around a chalice of wine and a loaf of bread,
           singing in that kind of sing-song Greek way.

I want you to see the house.
    Small.
    Cramped.
    The yard bare and hard.
    The paint on the doorframe is scratched and weathered
        and the grey wood shows through.
    A hole in the screen.
    There are no Oldsmobiles or Subarus in this neighborhood,
        just a few old heaps,
           and a couple of hulks
               sitting without tires
                  on concrete blocks.
  On the table there are some food stamps
    and a sack of children's clothing
        fresh from Goodwill.

And the house has *that* smell—
> that dirty,
>> greasy,
>>> stale
>>>> smell.

Do you get the picture?

And I want you to see the people.
> None of them in three-piece suits,
>> all-wool
>>> with pin-striped shirts
>>>> silk ties
>>>>> and wing-tip shoes.

> A man is there in chains,
>> wrists and ankles rubbed raw
>>> because he would not say,
>>>> "Caesar is Lord."
>>>>> Down on the ground,
>>>>>> in front of the statue,
>>>>>>> the best he could say is
>>>>>>> "Jesus is Lord."

> A black youth is there,
>> tired from walking the streets
>>> day after day
>>>> looking for a job.

> A mother is there,
>> trying to raise five kids
>>> alone
>>>> and on a welfare check.

> A refugee is there from Central America
>> in search of sanctuary,
>>>> constantly looking over his shoulder.

A family from the African desert is there,
   with arms and legs like sticks,
      their eyes hollow,
         their bellies bloated
           from hunger.

Someone is there
   whose face is half eaten away
      by cancer.
And a worker is there,
   fifty-eight years old,
      who came into the office one day
         and found a pink slip
         in the mailbox.

Do you get the picture?

This is a church of people on the outs,
      people who live on the margin of society,
         who are like the rubbings of the eraser,
         pushed over to the edge.

For all the world,
   they look weak,
   powerless,
      alienated,
         as if they could go
           right under the jackhammer of
           history
              and no one would notice,
             or care.

And then, in the smoky light of the lamps,
is one *like* a human being.
But from the way this figure is dressed,
and the things that surround him,
we know he is more
than an ordinary person.

He is clothed in a long white robe,
and in the ancient world
a long robe
was a garment
of the powerful,
an ancient equivalent
of the three-piece suit.

Around his breast is a golden girdle,
another symbol of power and authority
Head and hair white as well,
white as snow,
a luminescence of the resurrection,
a luminescence of heaven.

Eyes like flames of fire,
the fire that Moses saw at the burning bush,
the fire that burned the commandments into stone at
Sinai,

the fire that bolted down from heaven on Mt. Carmel.

Fire: characteristic of the appearance of God
such that to be in the presence of God
is like being in the presence of fire.

Feet like burnished bronze,
>   the same bronze that Ezekiel saw
>   when God came riding
>   across the storm-winds of history.

In his right hand,
>   he holds the seven stars
>   which we soon learn
>   are the seven churches.
From his mouth, a sharp two-edged sword,
>   an instrument of combat,
>   but coming from his mouth
>   it can hardly be a brutal weapon
>   with which to bludgeon and dismember
>   his enemies;
>   no, it can only be one thing:
>   the word of God.
>   How does he do battle
>   with the principalities and powers?
>   With tanks and missles?
>   No, with the word of preaching.

Add them all up:
>   robe
>   girdle
>   bronze
>   sword
>   the sun shining in full strength.
Add them all up and what are they?
Images of power.

This, you see, is the conquering Christ,
    the powerful, cosmic ruler
        who has fought the battle of life
        and won.

    What does Caesar look like
        compared to the conquering Christ?
    And what can any Caesar do to those
        who know this Christ?

Later in the book of Revelation,
    we will see that this cosmic Christ
        exercises power
            with the gentleness of the lamb.
    And we will see that the victory of the cosmic Christ
        was won on the cross.
    And we will learn that the sovereign power of God
        is revealed in the weakness
            of the lamb who was slain,
                and that the robes of his servants
                have been washed clean
                    in the blood of the lamb.

    But first,
        John's church sees him
            like the sun shining in full strength
                looking out over the world
                    with eyes of flaming fire.
    And when those eyes look into ours,
        they can set us aflame
            exposing the Caesars of this world
                in their cheap glitter
                    and setting the fire of God
                        to burning in our hearts,

the fire of God's living presence,
the fire of God's passionate love,
the fire of God's will for justice,
the fire that can never be crushed
out.

I want you to see Charles,
    out of the housing development
        for the first time.
He walks up to the window
    of the motion picture theater
        and the clerk
            looks
                right
                    past
                        him
            and motions to the people behind
                to come on up.
You'd think the clerk could see Charles
    six feet tall
    in a U.S. Army uniform
    beautiful black skin.
But no,
    she looks
        right
            past.
Can you see Charles now,
    thirty years later
        behind his desk at the Multi-Service Center,
            looking with his soft, glowing eyes
                into the eyes of every runaway youth
                into the eyes of every drunk off the street
                into the eyes of every city council member
                into the eyes of every John Bircher?

I want you to see Tom,
    getting on the plane
        at 6:30 a.m.
carrying a backpack with his clothes
        and a suitcase filled with medicines.
His ticket: Nicaragua
        where he is going as a Witness for Peace.
You wouldn't think it
        just to look at him:
            tall
            thin
            healthy
            a yuppielike haircut
            stylishly modest clothes
            and an M.B.A.

        He even had a job once
            ordering all the loose parts
                for the biggest hospital bed maker
                in the western world.
        He called himself, "The Widget King."

He's been worried.
Should he go:
        He's got responsibilities at his job.
        He'll use up all his vacation.
        His wife is pregnant.
He's been worried.
Does he have it in him
        to go to Central America
            and live in hovels
                high up in the mountains
                where the Contras come across?

He read a news clipping to us one time,
    which described the Contras coming across the border,
        bursting into a village,
           setting fire to the huts,
        poisoning the well
        putting the barrel of a rifle
                into the mouth of the local mayor
                    and leaving it for six hours
              kicking pregnant women in the belly
              with their combat boots.

But here he is,
    bags packed,
        passport in hand,
           getting on the plane
              to spend two weeks in the mountains
                because the Contras stay away—
              most of the time—
                when U.S. citizens
                  are in the area.
        A Witness for Peace.

And when he looks back to wave,
    you can just catch it
        in his eyes,
           the fire.

I want you to see Ed Hively,
    eighty-three years old,
        lying in the bed in intensive care.

He hasn't always been there.
When he was young he was in the navy

and in his pictures you can see him:
swarthy
muscled
white-capped Ed.
"Did you ever smell the sea at night?"
he asked me once.
"Smells like God."
And when he was middle aged,
he followed the harvest
from Texas to Canada,
year after year after year,
working every day from dawn to dark,
in the spring rain,
in the summer heat,
in the fall chill.

And now here he is,
in the intensive care room,
alone in the world,
kept alive by machines

a stroke slicing through his right side,
leaving his leg and arm stiff as pipes,
his eye pinched shut
his mouth twisted in a
grotesque smile.

He is sleeping
I go up to the bed,
reach across through the maze of tubes,
take his left hand in mine
and give it a squeeze.

And then he stirs,
    and locks my hand in his with a vicelike grip,
        and his good eye comes open,
            barely,
            and do you know what I see?
            Do you know what I see?

            Yes, you know.

            I see the fire.
            I see…the…fire.

THE GOGGLES OF EASTER

Cornish R. Rogers

In the Gospel according to Luke, Jesus reminds the disciples when he appeared to them after the resurrection that they should have known that he was going to rise from the dead, for he said, "Everything written about me in the law of Moses, the prophets, and the psalms must be fulfilled." He went on to remind them further that "it is written, that the Messiah is to suffer and to rise from the dead on the third day." He showed them that the resurrection is anticipated in many parts of the scriptures—that what was written in Moses and the prophets and the psalms was of one accord with the gospel (Luke 24:44–53).

Sometimes when you look back you wonder why we did not see it before. We have celebrated the resurrection. And I want to suggest to you this morning that, from the vantage point of Easter, we can see that the whole Bible breathes of the coming of the Messiah and the establishment of the final reign of God. And it is because of Easter that we suddenly see what God was driving at throughout the scriptures. In his book *The Great Code* Northrop Frye says something astounding. He says that the Exodus is the only thing that really happens in the Old Testament and everything else is merely a commentary on that great freedom song of Moses. He goes on to suggest that Moses' organization of the Israelites into twelve tribes finds its antitype in the apostles, that the passage through the Red

---

Cornish R. Rogers is professor of pastoral ministry at the School of Theology at Claremont, California.

Sea signifies baptism, that manna signifies the Sermon on the Mount. In all the Gospels, the passion and death of Jesus are centered on the Passover. The Last Supper is the Passover meal. The Crucifixion is the journey through the desert, and the Resurrection is victory over Israel's enemies. The force of the Bible, according to Frye, is *centripetal.*[1]

Of course, everyone does not agree with Northrop Frye, and we have come to appreciate the danger of seeing either the Hebrew scriptures or New Testament as prelude or postlude to the other. Nevertheless, we know that resurrection/new life is a pervasive and powerful biblical theme, and I believe that the experience of Easter sheds light on the whole story of God's plan for redeeming the world.

I am told that there was a set of goggles, manufactured by some engineers, that helped some of the soldiers during World War II and some of the woodmen who worked in the forest at night to be able to see even in the dark. Apparently these goggles are constructed in such a way that they focus whatever light exists (and you know light exists even in the darkness, even though we cannot see it— light from the stars, light from under the doorsill of a dark room, refracted light that does not seem to dispel the darkness for our naked eye). With those goggles the little light available is focused in such a way that the person who wears those goggles can see as if it were day. And so, they enabled some of our armed forces to engage in night battle, and also enabled people who worked in forests at night to be able to see.

I like to think of Easter in that way. I like to think of Easter as a pair of goggles that we use to focus the light, so that we can see as we ought to see. And I want to say briefly just three things about that.

The first thing is this: the Easter goggles help us to see that there is beauty even in ugliness. And this was brought home to me by an article I read in *Christianity and Crisis*, in which Robert MacAfee Brown wrote a review of praise for a book written by Mr. Alan Paton, the famous South African author. The book is called *Ah, But Your Land Is Beautiful*, and the theme of the book has to do with a lot of the difficulties between the races in that star-crossed country. Mr. Paton, while he is very sympathetic to those who are oppressed, is still very realistic in his novels, and does not paint a picture that does not conform to reality. And so in this book he tells it as it is, but yet somehow is able to make it beautiful—at least the possibilities are beautiful. The title of his book implies that even though you think the political condition of a country may be ugly, the land of South Africa is beautiful. But he works his themes in such a way that he demonstrates that what makes South Africa beautiful, if there is any beauty in it, is not the land alone, but a beauty of the people who stand up, the people who are willing to suffer, the people who are willing to rise above their suffering, the people who give of themselves and sacrifice themselves for others. And so Brown wrote a review of this book in which he says,

> Ah, but your book is beautiful, Mr. Paton. A beautiful book about ugliness, how can that be? How do you continue to find within the sordid, those gleams of the sublime that sometimes redeem, for moments at least, the ugliness that always threatens to destroy them?…How do you keep alive the sounds of hope when one by one they seem to be drowned out by the stronger sounds of orchestrated evil?[2]

And he goes on to conclude that "the beauty of your land is not finally a beauty in the field where the titahoya sings, but a beauty in the hearts of men and women who, standing in the midst of the ugliness of injustice, refuse to accept its power over them."[3]

I could not help, when I read it, but say to myself: "That's what the gospel reveals in us. That's what Easter illumines for us, the possibility of the beautiful in the midst of the ugly, and that things can be beautiful, even though the situation is ugly."

Maya Angelou, who is a poet and dancer and writer and a real Renaissance woman, describes her early life in Arkansas. She said she really had a tough childhood because she was not only black as a child, but she was also ugly. And to be black and ugly in Arkansas was to suffer tremendously. She said she was scorned and segregated by the whites and laughed at by the blacks because she was such a gawky child. She said that even at her mature age now, she still has those scars and lives with those scars, but she said, "At one time I was resentful of those scars, but now, before I write a poem, in order to prime my creative juices, I scrape my pen across those scars to sharpen the point."[4] I think it is because of those Easter goggles that it is possible to derive beauty from ugliness. Easter not only reveals that, but also reveals hope in the midst of a fearful situation. The scripture that was read to you this morning from Revelation really describes the way in which the beleaguered Christians at the end of the first century were able to face the ordeals that came upon them when they were persecuted by the Romans. The writer of the book, John of Patmos, told his people that he was taken up into heaven and saw how the end came. And he saw that eventually they would be victorious, and he came back and described the ordeals they must suffer, but also the victory that was promised. And he suggested that victory is already at hand, for it has already happened in heaven; it just had not been translated into earthly forms yet. And because of that, those persons were able to endure the ordeals. When you read that whole book, you discover that there is a very sordid description of violence and murders committed against the faithful, but in the midst of that, they stop and worship and praise God, for they anticipate the coming victory, as if the victory had already occurred. In those intervening worship services and praises to God throughout that book, they derive strength enough to meet the next ordeal.

Alternation between suffering and joy is the Christian lifestyle. Whenever we take on the mantle of Christ we will experience some suffering, but we will also experience joy. The beleaguered Christians of the first century employed that lifestyle in order to face the horrible portents of the Apocalypse.

The second affirmation has to do with how, under the light of Easter, things "add up" differently, thus providing hope where none appeared before. A minister friend of mine was surprised one Sunday afternoon watching a tennis match on television in which his hero was losing badly, only to hear on the radio in another room that his hero had won the match! It had been a delayed telecast! He said it reminded him of the essence of Christian hope; the "assurance of things hoped for" even while he was experiencing the ordeal of the present.

Letty Russell, a theologian at Yale University, suggests in her book *Growth in Partnership* that it is from that Easter light, from those goggles through which you can bring light to focus, that you discover that God has a way of doing arithmetic that is different from ours. And she calls it "God's new math."[5] I remember having been a physics major in college when I used to help my son with all of his third grade mathematics until the new math came out. Then I discovered that the new math just did not "add up" like the math I was used to. Fortunately my spouse was an elementary school teacher and had to attend workshops on how to teach the "new math." I soon found myself to be the only one in my home who did not understand the simple arithmetic of the new math.

But Letty Russell goes on to say that there is a new math that God has put into the world since Easter. For instance, things do not add up calculatorlike in God's new math; talents that are used multiply instead of adding up. People who work only the last hour receive the whole day's wages along with the people who work for eight hours. Those who are lost are saved, and those who often are saved are lost. Many sheep are neglected to search for one. The poor are fed and the rich are sent empty away. And you just look at all the parables of Jesus, and you discover God's new math operating—not through the logic of possession but through the logic of grace. That is what Easter gives us through its goggles. After Easter, God's new math makes sense to us.

And finally, after Easter there is a sense that no matter what happens to us, all is well. It is partly due to that vision of John of Patmos, as he talked to those beleaguered Christians saying that all would be well, for the victory had been won in heaven. It is partly due to what I have just alluded to: God's new math and the sense of hope. It is partly due to the fact that the scriptures always speak of the resurrection, and we should have seen it before. But more specificially, it speaks of a sense that, though I live, though I suffer, though I die—all is well, because all is well with God.

I got a sense of that when my son was very young. He told me later that sometimes, after we sent him to bed pretty early and he woke up in the middle of the night, he would wonder where he was and feel kind of lonely, until he heard my snoring in the next room. And then he said, "All is well"—that he knew where he was and that everything was OK. Well, in a real sense that is what we really gain from Easter: the sense that God is in his heaven and therefore all's right with the world, that God has fulfilled his promises to his people, that God has conquered the last great enemy of life, which is death, and therefore all is well. "Do not be afraid," the text says, "I am the first and the last, and the living one. I was dead, and see, I am alive forever and ever."

Julius Lester, a young writer, has written an autobiography of his first thirty-five years of life, called *All Is Well*. He was a young activist, working with Stokeley Carmichael during the civil rights revolution and the Black Power movement afterward. He went to Cuba and met with Castro and visited all the radical-socialist governments of South America and Europe in a frantic search for an ideal society. He was also heavily involved in the Brownsville section of Brooklyn, with the attempt to gain community control over the public school systems there, and finally, at the age of thirty-five, was burned-out and tired and decided to leave and go to join Thomas Merton in the Trappist Monastery in Gethsemane, Kentucky. He stayed there for a while, and then at the end of the book, he is just about to leave the monastery and he writes these words:

> I am eager to leave, to go into the world; and more and more not be of it. I cannot save the world, I cannot change the world, all I can do is say, "Lord, here I am. Use me." To submit one's life to that divine will is not to find peace, but to struggle and suffer. God does not provide answers because there are no questions. There is only that divine presence. There is no other reality. No other world. So, it is time for me to go back and maybe, God will set me ablaze. If he does not, it is of no moment, for all is well.[6]

In the same sense, all is well after Easter. God has vindicated God's people, showed us the kingdom. Jesus is that apocalyptic figure that has now become the first citizen of that new kingdom, inviting us into it, so that new kingdom has already begun. Jesus has reassured his disciples that all is well, that it is possible to experience beauty in ugly situations, it is possible to have hope in despairing situations, and it is possible to experience joy in all situations. For all is well with God's promises, and that's what really counts, for it means that all can be well with us too.

I remember Henry Butterfield, an elderly member of my congregation some years ago in inner city Los Angeles. He was a reformed alcoholic and had come to the church to tell me how grateful he was to God for having seen him through his alcoholism. He asked me to give him the privilege of cleaning the sanctuary every Saturday for nothing. Every Saturday he faithfully came and cleaned the sanctuary; one Saturday I came and heard him as he cleaned, singing from the top of his voice, "All is well with my soul!"

I look upon him as the representative person who understands what Easter is about. It was not much later that he got cancer and was wasting away in the hospital. When I visited him I offered to pray with him, to which he replied: "You know, Rev., I don't ask God for anything any more, I just praise him. I just say, "Thank you, God, thank you, Jesus, for my life: and that's all I need. So when you pray, don't ask God for anything for me, just thank him." He died thanking God; he somehow found the goggles with which to see what little light there was, and he rejoiced over what he saw, and he died content.

You will find almost the same thing if you read the short stories of Isaac Bashevis Singer, the great Hebrew short-story writer. In one of his collections of short stories, he writes a story called "Joy," the story of Rabbi Banish, who loses his children to poverty and disease. His wife rails at him and says—what good is all his learning, all his meditations and all his prayer if he can't keep his children. None of this has protected his family from the inevitable disaster. The rabbi slips into melancholy, then into despair. Finally he calls in a neighbor, Abraham Mosher, and says, "The atheists are right, there is no justice, no judge, there's no one ruling the world. Evil, Disease, blood, bones, death—none of it can be justified."[7] But he suddenly noticed through the open windows the fruit trees in the orchard, the chirping of the birds, the slanting pillars of dust and tiny particles, vibrating, no longer matter and not yet spirit but reflecting rainbow hues, and Singer then wrote that at the depth of his suffering, the rabbi feels something else, that something in him was laughing. "As long as you breathe, you must breathe." At his own moment of death, the rabbi speaks a word of advice. He says simply, "One should always be joyous."[8]

Well, we who know and have experienced Easter have a special way of looking at life and we ought to be reminded from time to time that because of Easter, all is well. And now we don't have to be anxious and fearful. We can enter into all the dangerous and secular strivings of our time to work for justice and peace, to fight oppression wherever we find it, to feed the hungry, and to attack those systems that victimize people, knowing all the time, however, that no matter how successful or how unsuccessful we are, all is well. If we get nothing else from the Easter experience, that is enough. All is well.

Notes

[1]See Northrop Frye, *The Great Code* (New York: Harcourt Brace Jovanovich, 1982), pp. 72, 78-79, 131ff. See also Naomi Bliven's review of Frye's book in *The New Yorker*, 31 May 1982, pp. 104-106.

[2]Robert McAfee Brown, "An Improbable Beauty," *Christianity and Crisis*, 42:6, 12 April 1982, p. 97.

[3]*Ibid.*, p. 100.

[4]Maya Angelou, in an televised interview with Bill Moyers on the Public Broadcasting System series, "Creativity."

[5]Letty Russell, *Growth in Partnership* (Philadelphia: Westminster, 1981), pp. 32ff.

[6]Julius Lester, *All Is Well* (New York: Morrow, 1982), p. 319.

[7]Isaac Bashevis Singer, "Joy," *Collected Stories of Isaac Bashevis Singer* (New York: Farrar, Straus, Giroux, 1982), p. 30.

[8]*Ibid.*, p. 37.

📖 2:1–7; 3:14–22

I HAVE THIS AGAINST YOU

Joseph R. Jeter, Jr.

The phone call was brief and professional. I had not gotten the job. The committee had no qualms about my ability to comfort the afflicted, the caller told me, but there was some doubt about my ability—or will—to afflict the comfortable. There were a few more awkward pleasantries and he rang off, leaving me to ponder this deficiency in my ministry.

There was truth there. Afflicting the comfortable is not my strong suit. Since that day in the third grade when Billy Don Massey let it be known that he was going to beat the tar out of me, I have made a career out of avoiding conflict. I could have said, "Come, Billy Don, let us reason together," but instead I decided to spend the afternoon meditating in the cottonwood tree, spiritual sort that I am. Odds are I would have made a lousy prophet. But I do want to be a good minister, and I know that calls for a creative tension between the pastoral and the prophetic, the comfort and the challenge. And more than that I want to be Christian, which means struggling with the dual gifts of judgment and grace. But it is hard to be a minister. It is hard to be Christian. And it is job-losing hard to get people to hear what is surely true, that God loves us unconditionally, together with what is also surely true, that God is disgusted with our sin. How, then, are we to afflict the comfortable for the sake of the gospel?

Joseph R. Jeter, Jr. is Granville and Erline Walker associate professor of homiletics at Brite Divinity School, Texas Christian University, Fort Worth, Texas.

Chapters 2 and 3 of the book of Revelation consist of pastoral letters from the prophet John to seven churches of Asia Minor. They follow a highly structured form and all the messages are for all the churches. John's intention is to show the churches who and what they really are and to prepare them for his vision of the future. As a prophet, John wants his hearers to be able to draw a clear contrast between the world as it is, which includes them, and the new world that God is bringing into being, which may or may not include them.

You have just heard the bookends, the first and last of these letters, read for us. There are several familiar texts in them, from "I wish that you were either cold or hot," to "Listen! I am standing at the door, knocking." As we read them, we see these texts are a composite of praise and blame. John offers praise for the patient endurance in the midst of tribulation and criticizes those who have abandoned the path of faith. Why did John do that?

Think about it. What if there had been only praise? It does seem appropriate. Here is a group of little churches, struggling in the midst of an increasingly hostile culture, facing more and more intense persecution. Why not just wrap them in hugs and smother them with warm fuzzies? Why does he have to keep breaking into his narrative of praise with the words, "But I have this against you"?

William Holman Hunt was the most idolized painter of nineteenth-century England. A leader of the pre-Raphaelite school, Hunt chose religious themes for most of his paintings and traveled to the Near East so the settings for his works might be more authentic. Everywhere he went, Hunt was lionized. He was called the greatest Protestant painter ever. Critics said that what Bach did for music, Hunt did for art.[1] His most famous painting, called *Light of the World*, shows Christ standing with a lantern before a closed door. You have probably seen it. "Behold, I stand at the door and knock; if anyone hears my voice and opens the door, I will come in..." is engraved beneath the painting. The reaction was overwhelming. People stood in awe before the painting, deeply moved. Some claimed that it was a message from heaven and many conversions were reported. The painting went on a world tour that would have made Michael Jackson envious. It was reportedly seen by more than four-fifths of all the people living in Australia and New Zealand.[2] The praise for Holman Hunt rolled in.

And yet. The same Holman Hunt was frequently found in brothels where he could indulge one of his favorite pastimes—beating up women, even bragging to a friend that he had hurled one all the way across a room. He broke his engagement to a woman who loved him because he decided that she was "beneath" him. He married a relative of Evelyn Waugh named Fanny and forced her to model for him even when pregnancy left her too weak to stand. After she died in childbirth, he quickly married her sister Emily and abused her from day one.[3] In the midst of the apotheosis of the great Christian painter William Holman Hunt, could no one be found who would hold Hunt's misogyny up to him and say, "I have *this* against you"?

Why did John not simply shower the churches with love and praise? Because John was a prophet and prophets have very high standards. But also because people and churches, then and now, who become morally lax and spiritually lazy, who abandon the faith journey for a self-satisfied dwelling place veneered with the pretense of religion, and who continue to be told how wonderfully perfect they are, tend to sink in the mire of their own lethargy and sin. As Kazantzakis said, "When God raises a storm, woe to the one who pours oil into the sea,"[4] good words for us, as well as for Exxon.

Now, suppose that John had proffered only blame. Suppose that he had condemned and flayed the churches, offering no possibility of redemption. Suppose he had not said over and over again, seven times, "Let anyone who has an ear listen to what the Spirit is saying to the churches." Some believe John to be very harsh in these letters and yet justified. A preaching student had just finished reading Jonathan Edward's biting sermon "Sinners in the Hand of an Angry God," where humankind is pictured hanging by a gossamer thread over the fiery pit of hell. After some thought, the student wrote, "If I were God, I'd let 'em go."

Would you now? I remember sitting with a pastor at a large church assembly where speaker after speaker got up to lambaste us about our not doing enough for peace and justice. Finally, the pastor leaned over and said, "About the fifth time I get harassed on a subject, I just don't give a damn anymore." Why did John not simply castigate the churches, roll up a big ball of hell fire and damnation and let them have it? Because churches are a lot like children—they learn what they live. If a church lives with criticism, they learn to condemn. If a church lives with hostility, they learn to fight.[5]

Breece D'J Pancake is the unlikely name of a brilliant young writer who took the literary world by storm in the late 1970s, until he took his own life in 1979 at the age of twenty-seven. Why? Groping for an answer, one of his teachers wrote this:

Breece's favorite quotation was from the Bible—Revelation 3:15–16: "I know thy works, that thou art neither cold nor hot. Would that thou wert cold or hot! So then because thou art lukewarm, and neither cold nor hot, I will spew thee out of my mouth." This is a dangerous pair of verses. Untempered by other messages, by the gentler tones of voice of the Spirit, they can be a scourge.[6]

Yes, they can. And people are telling me that out in the communities right now there are religious groups using the book of Revelation as just such a scourge, developing among their members and especially their young people a pathological fear of God as someone who hates them and cannot wait to destroy them. The tragedy is that these groups, and Pancake, and so many others have missed the gentler tones of spirit that are right in the letters themselves! The blame is never soft-pedaled, that's true, but it is surrounded—kindness and praise in front, promise and glory behind. The blame is therefore limited, circumscribed; it has boundaries fore and aft. There is no original sin here. The churches were conceived in the love and sacrifice of Christ. And there is no endless punishment, for in front of them stands the promise of the coming reign of God. So the blame is limited: "I have this against you right now. Come on, people, get with it!" But the praise and promise are limitless, originating and coming to fulfillment in the boundless love of God.

The best example of this I know is found in the story of Jesus and the woman at the well (John 4). The story begins with an act of kindness. Jesus, a Jewish man, engages a Samaritan woman in dialogue, treating her, against the custom of the time, as an equal. And the story ends with tremendous promise, as Jesus announces to her the presence of the Messiah, "I am he, the one who is speaking to you." Jesus has already spoken to all manner of folk, including the religious leaders of the day. But the announcement of the promise inherent in the Messiah is reserved for this Samaritan woman. In front is kindness; behind is promise. In between, to quote from Peter, Paul, and Mary, "he told her everything she'd ever done."

We see it again and again. At the table, on the road to Emmaus, again on the road to Damascus, and in John's letters to the churches. The loving rebuke, circumscribed fore and aft, not an oxymoron, but a necessity for Christian growth. And we are not very good at it. Evangelical Joyce Lansdorf was a popular motivational speaker on the lecture circuit until she went through a very painful and difficult divorce a few years ago. Suddenly her speaking engagements were canceled and her invitations dried up; she had become a pariah among the very ones she had loved and served. She struggled through, but speaking about this later, she said that one thing she learned from this experience was that when people say to you, "I tell you this in Christian love," duck![7] I, like most pastors, have memories of sermons to my people that I thought were prophetic but that were, in reality, merely bitchy. No blessing, no promise, just criticism. I was a long time learning that the greatest judgment of all is the judgment of grace: "In the same night that we betrayed him, he took bread."[8] I wish that Breece Pancake could have learned it, too.

From the Hebrew prophets to Jesus to the prophet John and right into the present world, we see the prophetic model of ministry continue to unfold. Allan Boesak has found the book of Revelation to be an encouraging word for those who suffer in South Africa. In his words, the blessing that opens the book, "Grace to you and peace from him who is and who was and who is to come, ...and from Jesus Christ, the faithful witness, the firstborn of the dead, and the ruler of the kings of the earth" (1:4–5), is "a blessing beyond price to a fearful and persecuted church."[9] Remember: first the blessing.

In his ministry Boesak has stood against the racist policies of his government and has come again and again to this country with his message. "I have this against you, America. Your support of the South African government lengthens the dark night of our soul." Again, "I have this against you, churches. Your moral suasion lies unused and bankrupt at the time of our greatest need." And again, "I have this against you, universities. Your investment money pays for the guns that keep my people in subjection." He writes:

> Our children are shot in the street like dogs; our pregnant women are beaten and kicked by laughing soldiers....Those who struggle for justice, peace and genuine reconciliation on the basis of their Christian faith, are charged with treason and subversion, are banned and killed. Those who support apartheid, who abet the evil-doers in their evil, are rewarded with money and power. The upholders of apartheid and oppression, the killers of children, sit in parliament and call themselves "Servants of God." Their words are arrogant and blasphemous, for their power is not from the Living One, the God of Israel, but from the dragon, the deceiver and liar.[10]

Remember: after the blessing, comes the rebuke. All of us can understand and stand under Boesak's language, feel its sting and, one hopes, be prompted to action. (And now, in the face of personal problems, Boesak the rebuker knows rebuke himself.) But something has been missing. And that is why I am so touched by the reports that have come to me from the Encuentro gathering last May in San Antonio. Boesak stood up to speak, I am told, and voiced the same urgent critique as before, hammering away about struggle and accountability. He spoke of his ten-year-old son and others who have been harassed by police for carrying candles. But suddenly he stopped. And then, with measured words: "Someday, when all of this is over, my son will visit your country and when he does, he will not talk of apartheid and prison and broken families, but of schools and churches and new life."[11] Do you hear it? The promise now joins the blessing and the rebuke. And for Boesak, like his forebears in the faith, the prophetic circle is complete.

We have been called to ministry, the whole ministry. And part of that is the prophetic ministry, the ministry of "no" to things as they are, the ministry of afflicting the comfortable, the ministry of God's judgment and grace. Let us not shrink from this task that John has modeled for us so well. How shall we do it? "You are children of Christ that I love. Do not be afraid, because the new reign of God is coming. In between, and in order that you might both claim your heritage and stretch toward your destiny, I take a deep breath and speak in God's name, because you must know that 'I have this against you.'"

Come to think of it, I got the job. And so did you.

Notes

[1]P. T. Forsyth, *Religion in Recent Art* (New York: Edwin S. Gorham, 1902), pp. 154-155.

[2]Jeremy Maas, *Holman Hunt and the Light of the World* (London: Scolar Press, 1984), p. 190.

[3]Martin E. Marty, "A Portrait of the Artist as a Creep," *Context*, 15 September 1989, p. 4.

[4]Nikos Kazantzakis, *Russia*, trans. Michael Antonakes & Thanasis Maskaleris (Berkeley: Creative Arts Book Co., 1989), p. 1.

[5]Adapted from a rather well-known statement about raising children. I have seen it reproduced in various formats, but have been unable to document the source.

[6]John Casey, "Afterword," *The Stories of Breece D'J Pancake* (New York: Holt, Rinehart and Winston, 1984), p. 176.

[7]I have this story from Bryan Feille.

[8]See James Sanders, "In the Same Night," *God Has a Story, Too* (Philadelphia: Fortress Press, 1979), p. 94.

[9]Allan A. Boesak, *Comfort and Protest: The Apocalypse from a South African Perspective* (Philadelphia: Westminster Press, 1987), p. 50.

[10]*Ibid.*, pp. 100-101.

[11]This was told to me by Julie Pierce.

EVERYTHING IS GOING TO BE ALL RIGHT

M. Eugene Boring

Why is it that something inside us cringes a little at the words, "I am going to preach a sermon on the book of Revelation"? Is it because Revelation has always had a marginal place in the canon? This book comes at the end of the Bible not because it tells of the last things—eschatology is an integral part of many biblical books—but because it barely got in at all. As late as the fourth century Eusebius still lists it as both "accepted" and "disputed," saying that half the churches accept it, and half do not.[1] It was not admitted to the Bible of the Syrian church until the sixth century. When it finally did receive official canonical status, Christians and scholars of the stature of Martin Luther and his twentieth-century exponent, Rudolf Bultmann, though they could not reverse the decision of the church, declined to have Revelation in their personal canon. Multitudes of Christians of all denominations are "Lutheran" at this point. And John Calvin wrote commentaries on every book of the New Testament—except one.

Or are we uncomfortable with Revelation because some Christians have almost limited their Bible to Revelation, forever trying to pin 666 on someone, and predicting the imminent End while making a mint? So we decide that if they want Revelation, they can have it?

Could it be that we shun Revelation because, beneath our veneer of sophistication, we are still troubled by half-remembered

---

M. Eugene Boring is professor of New Testament at Brite Divinity School, Texas Christian University, Fort Worth, Texas.

fears of burning pits and primeval monsters that we thought we had put behind us, only to find that they still well up in the abyss within us, to haunt our dreams, our reading of Moby Dick, and dread of dying?

Or is it that long after our two-hundredth national birthday and all the media hype about getting the Statue of Liberty properly restored, we have finally decided to grow up, and renounce those hopes for utopia and the millennium that have dogged our national history? That hardy band that began on the East Coast and drove westward, with God and good conscience pushing the Indians out or under, has made it to the West Coast, to Alaska, Hawaii, and the moon, but the dream remains unfulfilled: the amber waves of grain have become a pawn in world politics; the purple mountains are paved over and violated with sewer pipes; smog and jets clog the spacious skies; and our good remains uncrowned with brotherhood or sisterhood from sea to shining sea. We will put escapist dreams behind us, grow up, and accept the world as it is. And get nervous or mad when the book of Revelation is opened.

Let's face it. Revelation is so pathetically unrealistic. *"Everything* is going to be *all* right" is unrealistically extravagant. Wouldn't it be better to say, *"If* we really work at it, *maybe* some things might get a *little* better"? Perhaps this lack of realism is the ground of our discontent with this book. A social and political crisis threatened the churches of the Roman province of Asia in 96 A.D. The government is threatening to act against the Christian movement. A test case, Antipas of Pergamum, is already through the courts, and Antipas is condemned and executed (2:13). John is a pastor who has a tender and responsible relationship to his people in the crisis they are facing. He could have done something realistic, something that might have actually helped: organize a lobby, raise funds for the support of Antipas' widow and children, or, if all he can do is write, he could at least write an explanation of the Christian movement for Roman leaders, as did Luke his contemporary and the later Apologists. Do we cringe because here in Revelation we are faced with one of those who, in a situation where people have real problems, refuse to take any responsibiltiy for the world, set up their "Jesus is Coming Soon" sign, and speak of pearly gates and golden streets?

Or does our reluctance at hearing the message of Revelation spring from our fear of what the book might say to us? Do we suspect that underneath the gaudy wrapping with its weird pictures is not a present at all, but a bomb that will make a shambles of the playground we have constructed for ourselves?

We are made uncomfortable by the claim of the first sentence of our text: "After this I looked, and there in heaven a door stood open! And the first voice, which I had heard speaking to me like a trumpet, said, 'Come up here, and I will show you what must take place after this'" (4:1). John claims that the voice of Jesus still speaks. When we face social and political situations where Christians have to decide what to do, we have learned how to handle them: have a discussion group or a panel discussion, with a wide-but-not-too-wide spectrum of views presented, and let each person make up his or her own mind. We are offended by people like John, who stride in with their "Thus says the Lord," and we have good biblical precedent for telling them to go back to Judah, and to eat bread and prophesy there (Amos 7:10–13). It is a dangerous idea this John has. A Jesus who is back there in the Bible and tradition is, if not domesticated, at least manageable, and we sovereign hermeneuts are skilled at deciding how to "apply" his teaching to our situation. But what if Jesus still speaks?

And it is not just the way John speaks. The content of his purported revelation makes us squirm as well. "I will show you what must take place after this" (4:1). He claims the ultimate future is already decided; he claims to know how it is all going to turn out. Let us be clear: John does not pretend to predict what is going to happen today or tomorrow, but claims that the goal of all our tomorrows is—*already decided!* Human beings are still free and responsible, but according to John, history is finally in God's hands, and, in the words of Reinhold Niebuhr, he will bring it to a worthy conclusion.

It may be a nice idea, but it is full of problems too, and just as we are about to lay some hard questions on this would-be prophet, he refuses to be pinned down and speak in clear statements, but presents us with a surrealistic picture and a collection of hymns. We stand before this one who claims to have information from heaven, and confront him with the facts of life: the whimpers of the little starving children of Africa and India too weak even to cry, and we want a straight answer, an explanation. And we get: pictures and songs. (Remember those legal minds who stood before another Jew when he talked about caring for the neighbor, and asked their calculating question, "Yes, but who is my neighbor?" He told them a story.) Not the least of the scandalous things about Revelation is that we ask for a diagram and get a mind-blowing picture; we ask for a logical explanation, and get a song.

But we have come this far. Why not indulge him and his picture?

"There in heaven stood a throne, with one seated on the throne!" There is a control room for the universe, and it is not vacant. Spaceship Earth has a Mission Control, a reference point for all that happens here. This is John's picture. Does it exist only in the mind?

> You know, more and more I think that for many years I looked at life like a case at law, a series of proofs. When you're young you prove how brave you are, or how smart; then, what a good lover; then, a good father; finally, how wise, or powerful, or what-the-hell ever. But underlying it all, I see now, there was a presumption. That I was moving on an upward path toward some elevation, where—God knows what—I would be justified, or even condemned—a verdict anyway. I think now that my disaster really began when I looked up one day—and the bench was empty. No judge in sight.[2]

For Arthur Miller, there ought to be an Occupied Throne, but there isn't, and life is a puzzle and a disappointment. John's picture, in the face of asburdly more evil circumstances, dares to eliminate the gap between "ought" and "is." Someone is in the driver's seat of the cosmos.

"And around the throne is a rainbow." We have read Revelation before, and we know what a deluge of catastrophes it portrays. But Revelation is also the only New Testament book to take up the Old Testament sign of hope, the emblem of God's convenant with the earth and all life upon it. The blood and thunder are there in Revelation, as they are in the world. But John sees them framed by the sign of hope.

"Twenty-four elders...with golden crowns on their heads." Whatever there may be of astrology and mythology in this reference, John probably wants us to see the whole People of God (twelve tribes, twelve apostles) portrayed here. And before we are too eager to consider the crowns a bit of otherworldly Johannine ostentation, we might remember that the crown is the mark of the Christian who has given his or her life in the real this-worldly persecution of Domitian (2:10).

"Seven flaming torches, which are the seven spirits of God." These are not ornamental accoutrements of the Throne Room, but the spirits that are sent out to all the earth, the Spirit by which God is present to all creation, and it to him. Here we have no isolated scene, no Greek gods cavorting on Olympus far removed from both our cries of pain and the joyful sounds of our parties.

"And in front of the throne there is something like a sea of glass, like crystal." Everyone in the Bible knows that the sea has always been the anti-world, anti-creation force, pushed to the boundaries of creation "in the beginning," but still there, still hostile. You can walk down to the fragile border that separates water and land and see the restless sea still gnawing away at the edges of the earth, held at bay, but not resigned. But in John's picture of the behind-the-scenes Real Future World, the darkest forces of the universe are, in God's presence, as calm as glass.

"Four living creatures." The picture already seems complete enough: God and us. Why these pictures of all forms of animal life? Because John is concerned with more than a picture of how our existential inner selves are related to God (another reason we don't like apocalyptists—they aren't anthropocentric). This is a picture of creation, and it is a creation-song that breaks out:

> You are worthy, our Lord and God
> to receive glory and honor and power,
> for you created all things,
> and by your will they existed and were created.
>   Revelation 4:11

Here is something to sing about, a response to our deep question, the question that plagued the persecuted church of Asia in the 90s, the question that plagues everyone who perceives that things in the world have somehow gone wrong. The question: "Why?"

I have met this *Ur-question* not only in Heidegger and Tillich ("Why is there something and not nothing?"), and from the crosses that dot our landscape ("My God, why. . . ?"), but in ordinary conversation with ordinary people. As a pastor, I was taking my turn as hospital chaplain. While dutifully calling on a man slightly injured in a traffic accident that made only the fifth page, he interrupted my opening pleasantries with "Pastor, can you tell me why?" Maintaining my best pastoral care tone, I countered, none too profoundly, "Why *what?*" "Why *anything?*" He was no philosopher by disposition, just one who lived, and dared to look beneath the surface of life.

Bursting from John's picture comes a response to that mostly unspoken question buried within us all. Why anything? Because one God created all things and willed that they exist! For John, it is not something to be explained, but to be sung about. He will have no atheistic cop-out, no polytheistic cop-out (much popular talk of the devil and angels is a disguised polytheism), no semi-God cop-out offering a finite god who does the best he can like the rest of us, but who is subject to the same process, and stands by wringing his hands when the going gets too tough. No. John invites us to join in the hymn to the Creator because we live in a world that is no accident, but is the willed creation of the one God.

But just as we are tempted to join in the song to the Creator, we look again at the world, and John's answer becomes itself a problem. *This* world is a *creation*? If one almighty God is in charge of history, how account for the parade of misery, history's pageant of suffering? Augustine posed it cleanly for all of us: God either cannot, or will not, make an end of the evil of the world. If he can but will not, is he good? And if he will but cannot, is he God?[3]

Even if accepted at face value, John's vision up to this point (through 4:11) simply poses the problem. If there is one God, the Father Almighty, Maker of heaven and earth, this itself is not necessarily good news, and by itself solves nothing, as everyone from Marcion onward has known. *What is the will of such a God?* This is the issue. John is bothered by this, too. His eyes are fastened on the sealed book in the hand of the One seated on the throne. There is the answer. There is One who is responsible for the universe and its history. But his will, his purpose for his creation, is a sealed book. Could we be in the hands of a capricious tyrant? Even a sadistic monster? Who can say? John does not join in the singing. He cries.

Comes the denouement! The Messiah appears at the culmination of history, reveals God and acts for him. "Do not weep. See, the Lion of the tribe of Judah, the Root of David, has conquered, so that he can open the scroll and its seven seals" (5:5). This is the value of apocalyptic thinking, not just in Revelation and Daniel, but in Paul and Jesus. It provides a framework in which we can affirm (1) the world is the good creation of the good God, (2) the evil in the world is real, but temporary, for (3) at the End, God will destroy evil. Apocalyptic calls us to look for a solution not just upward, to some ideal world, not inward, to find my true self, but forward to God's future. His kingdom will come, his will will be done on earth, as it is in heaven.

John expresses this hope in the venerable, violent image of the Lion. Immediately upon entering the biblical world, we begin to see signs: "You are in Lion country." An oppressed people, battered throughout their history by this empire and that, declared their faith that such injustice could not be the last word about the way the world is, and often expressed their hopes for the coming deliverance in the expectation of the Lion-like one to come who would devour the enemies and vindicate his mistreated people. It is a daring faith, a risky hope—but what could be more right?

Our own time knows this hope too. As we draw near to that religious center of our culture where all our fantasies and frustrations are acted out in myth and ritual—I refer to the football stadium, we are met with placards and banners urging deserved violence upon the foes. The Detroit Lions have been in the cellar of the NFL. Their star fullback has been hurt. But he is promised to return in power and great violence, rougher than ever. The crowd is on its feet, we are led in the introductory ritual, and are full of righteous expectation that the long-promised Day is about to begin. Our hearts swell with anticipated pleasure at the slaughter to come, as the cheerleaders begin their chant: "Let's hear it for the Detroit *Lambs.*"

John takes over the apocalyptic framework, but with one mind-wrenching swerve, he fills in the Lion-slot in our mythology of "justice" with the Lamb. This is because John believes that the Messiah is Jesus of Nazareth, the crucified one. This cross is his conquest and his victory.

That we believe in a Messiah does not make us Christian. Prior to and aside from Christianity, many have looked for the solution to the evil in the world in some great figure to come at the End and destroy evil. It is Christian to believe that the Messiah is Jesus, that the crucified Man for Others is the ultimate One of history, who takes the sealed book from the hand of God and reveals to us who God is and what his purpose for the world is. Lamb power. Love power. The final word about God and the world.

Not only outsiders, but "Bible-believing" Christians have squirmed under this picture, and have found ways to avoid it. The most common escape hatch has been to see the Lamb as only penultimate, and the Lion as still ultimate. "Jesus has already been here as the Lamb, but when he comes back, it will be as the Lion." This view does not believe that *Jesus* is the Christ, that the content of the Jewish category "Christ" is to be filled in by who Jesus of Nazareth actually was. Jesus was only God's next-to-last word. Love is only a temporary strategem; God's ultimate nature is still violence. This is finally a sub-Christian view.

To say "Jesus is the Christ" is to affirm that in Jesus we meet God's final word to us, that at the end of our own personal history, and at the end of the world's history, the One with whom we have to do is the same One met in the crucified teacher of Nazareth. The scandal and challenge of the Christian faith is that the love met in Jesus, love that is willing to suffer and even die at the hands of evil, is the ultimate power of the universe, and shall finally prevail. There is no "Plan B."

✳ ✳ ✳

By the hospital bed, outside the divorce court, in the midst of the loneliness of another cocktail party, the eyes of our fellow human beings turn to us with questions they dare not even express. We want to say, and sometimes even do say, "Everything is going to be all right." Even Anne Frank wrote in her dairy just a few days before their attic apartment was finally discovered by the Nazis and they were all carted off to die at Auschwitz, "I think it will all come out right." What is this we say to each other? At best, trite? At worst, a lie? While we're trying to make up our minds, the song breaks out again. It starts with the four living creatures around the throne, then spreads in concentric circles to the elders, is taken up by the uncountable numbers of angels, and spreads until

I heard every creature in heaven and on earth and under the earth and in the sea, and all that is in them, singing,

"To the one seated on the throne and to the Lamb
be blessing and honor and glory and might
forever and ever."

Revelation 5:13

✳ ✳ ✳

Why do we cringe, why is it that the message of Revelation is so hard to hear? Because in the midst of our situation, it confronts us with the scandalous good news that the one who died as the victim of the world's evil is the Victor, and that the one revealed in his life and death is the God and savior of all creation.

From the midst of my cool, jaded affluence, I can give you twenty reasons why John is a fool. And in the midst of the loneliness and absurdity of his unjust situation, he paints a picture larger than the world that says, "Go ahead and celebrate. Everything is going to be all right." Heaven already joins in the song of celebration. Finally all creation will. We are given permission not only not to cry, but to join in the singing. And we can say to each other, not as a banal nonstatement but as life-giving word: everything is going to be all right.

Notes

[1]Eusebius, *Ecclesiastical History*. 3.25.
[2]Arthur Miller, *After the Fall* (New York: Bantam Books, 1964) pp. 4-5.
[3]Augustine, *Confessions*, VII. 5.

THE STRENGTH OF WEAKNESS

Ron O'Grady

In 1974 President Marcos of the Philippines decided that some left-wing Christians were becoming too radical. He encouraged the military to take a harder line against activist clergy and there followed a wave of arrests and "disappearances." Many Christians went underground and a strong network of supporters within the country and overseas gave assistance to the priests, nuns, and laypeople who were under threat.

It was in this context that some of us rediscovered the book of Revelation. The symbolic language of a people facing oppression suddenly became as relevant in the twentieth century as it was in the first. People of strong religious faith who faced the possibility of being tortured and killed felt an instant affinity with Christians in a similar situation several centuries earlier.

When they opened their Bible at chapter 5 of the book of Revelation, everything fell into perspective and there was a new hope.

Nobody had to explain the symbols to these people. They knew when they read the first words about "the one who was seated on the throne," that it referred to God. The thrones of this world are temporary and the dictators and rulers who sit upon them will not survive.

Ron O'Grady is a minister of the Associated Churches of Christ in New Zealand and former associate general secretary of the Christian Conference of Asia. Vice-chairperson of the Asian Christian Art Association, he lives in Auckland, New Zealand.

Come with me now and see the rest of this remarkable chapter in the setting of our contemporary world.

God on the throne has a scroll that is sealed (v. 1). It is the message that God has for us. It is the truth about life here on earth. Since it is God's message it will answer our deepest questions: "Why is there so much suffering?" "Why does evil triumph?" "Why does not God, or someone, open the scroll and tell us the meaning of it all?"

A strong angel steps forward (v. 2) and asks whether there is someone worthy to open the scroll but there is nobody able to do so. Not Billy Graham or Pope John Paul. Not the World Council of Churches or the Little River Church of God. Nobody has that direct line with God that enables them to go directly to the throne and give the absolute answers to our human condition (v. 3).

Throughout history it has been the same. We honor our fellow human beings, treat them as gurus and make them saints, but in the end we discover that they are not gods. The scroll remains closed.

I wept (v. 4). I wept because there was nobody to open the scroll and explain it to me. I wept one day in Bangladesh after their war of independence when I walked among piles of bodies of women and children who had been the innocent victims of weeks of brutal fighting. I have wept before the television screen at the sight of starving children in the Sudan.

Is there no one able to open the scroll and help me make sense of what I am seeing?

Then a wise old man came up and touched me on the shoulder and told me to stop crying (v. 5).

It is always amazing to see the number of times in our young lives when the experience and wisdom of an old man or old woman has helped us to make sense of an otherwise impossible situation.

"Don't worry," says this old man, "the Lion of Judah has conquered and he will open the seal." Well done! Wonderful news! That is exactly the message I have been looking for. It is also the language I understand. The media is always talking about strong leadership. In the church as in politics we seek people who are lions. Kings of the concrete jungle. Let's hear it for the lion!

It is at this moment that the Bible confronts us with what must surely be one of the most startling paradoxes of all time. After this majestic buildup, when all on earth has failed and only a strong, mighty and powerful lion-figure can save us, we look to the throne with tremendous expectancy and what do we see (v. 6)?

"I saw…a Lamb standing as if it had been slaughtered." Dear God! What is happening? We turned to view the lion and instead see this dying lamb.

I don't know how much power this symbolism has to those of you who come from the city. In New Zealand, where I live, we still have a predominantly rural economy. Though our human population is about 3 million, we have a population of over 70 million sheep. You can see who runs the country.

We have grown up with sheep. Each spring, at the lambing season, these fragile, helpless creatures come into the world in the millions. The hill sides are bursting with newborn lambs. And what weak, stupid, and helpless animals they are. They are totally dependent. Changes in the weather may mean instant death. Separation from the mother is equally fatal. Orphaned lambs are often hand fed by farmer's children with a baby bottle.

If you are looking for a symbol of all that is weak and helpless, you would not find anything better than the tiny, woolly lamb.

How can a lamb possibly be the one who will be able to go to the throne of God and reveal the mystery of life to us all?

Slowly the lamb moves forward and takes the scroll from the hand of God (v. 7). All over heaven there is a sigh of relief and the saints of the ages shout with happiness that the lamb has succeeded when all others have failed.

"Worthy is the Lamb," they shout (v. 12).

It is the great paradox of our Christian faith that it is the lamb who speaks to us of God's simplicity and compassion.

The lion is generals and dictators and wife-beaters—the lamb is peacemakers, lovers of nature, and the gentle folk.

The lion is the ruthless businessman, the wealthy property developer—the lamb is the laughter in the slum and the poor widow who can only afford two farthings to put in the offering.

The lion is war—the lamb is peace.
The lion is aggressor—the lamb is victim.
The lion will die—the lamb is God.

And that is why, in the end, the lamb will triumph. Despite all the evidence to the contrary, and despite the apparent strength and power of the lion, it is the lamb who holds the secret of the universe and who must ultimately triumph.

The victory does not belong to the great and powerful people of history but to the simple people who go through life showing love and compassion to those in need. They are people without public fame who do not make the headlines but whose simple faith, love of beauty, and concern to assist others make them the true descendants of the lamb.

It is their very humility that gives them a power that is finally greater than that of any oppressive force.

For if these same simple people are faced with oppression, whether in the small circle of domestic life or as a result of a political dictatorship, they will oppose the evil power of the lion with a quiet determination that is impossible to destroy.

You cannot kill such people. You cannot neutralize their power.

The last verses of chapter 5 of Revelation contain two majestic songs of praise to the lamb. Scholars maintain that these were actual hymns sung by the early church. The records of the persecution of Christians by successive Roman emperors state that many of the Christians walked into the arena of death singing hymns so it is logical to assume that the hymns of chapter 5 were among the hymns of those early martyrs.

What great hymns they are. None of your modern sentimental hymns that have become so self-centered and self-indulgent. These were real hymns of praise.

> Worthy is the Lamb that was slaughtered
> to receive power and wealth and wisdom and might
> and honour and glory and blessing!
> Revelation 5:12

They were the hymns of people who knew the source of real power and wisdom. Against all the seeming might of Rome simple people dared to stand up and sing that the weak and fragile little lamb that was slain was the ultimate conqueror of the world.

Today, the forces of evil continue to exert a powerful influence on the thoughts and attitudes of people in every country. Sometimes the lion is so powerful that we tremble for ourselves and for future generations.

Then it is time to turn back to Revelation and find the truth that it is in the humility of the lamb that ultimate power resides.

> It is the Lamb of God who takes away the sin of the world.
> It is the Lamb of God who gives us peace.
> To the Lamb be blessing forever.

GOOD SHOW

William H. Willimon

It was meant to be a put-down, a remark aimed to put me in my place. In a way, it did, but not as he intended. Why is Duke Chapel so often full when many university chapels or local churches are so often empty? He said, "Well, Duke Chapel puts on such a show on Sunday morning. And there are always those who want church to be nothing but a good show."

The buildings, the windows, the great choir, music from two organs, and sermons by two adorable ministers—Humph! It's all just a show. And I, not one to be put down without a fight said, "So what's wrong with a show—if it is a very, very *good* show?"

I hesitate to speak for God—although I do so regularly from this pulpit—but I can't think of any reason why God should be opposed to a Sunday morning show—unless it's not a good show.

Tell me, as you leave after service today, "Good show!" I won't take offense. Our director of music will be positively pleased.

We're putting on a show for God. Why do you think we're all dressed up and the candlesticks are polished and the linen is pressed and the timpani are tuned? We're doing it for the benefit of a God who enjoys our prayers, our hymns, our trumpets and "loud clashing symbols" (Psalm 150). If God didn't seek and enjoy our praise, thanksgiving, and petition, we wouldn't be here and this building could be subdivided into faculty offices.

As Kierkegaard said, here is Sunday morning theater in which God is the admiring audience and we—choir, preacher, musicians,

William H. Willimon is minister to the university and professor of the practice of Christian ministry at Duke University, Durham, North Carolina.

congregation—are on stage doing our best to make it a show worth watching.

But we're at a show in a twofold sense. For we are not only performing for God: *God is also performing for us.* The Germans have a word for worship—*Gottesdienst.* It means "God's service" in the twofold sense of the service we render to God and the service God renders to us. There are many Sundays when you are busy singing, praying, listening to God only to find that (surprise!) God is listening to you. You came here depressed and leave exhilarated. You wander in, plop down in the pew, only to sail forth with new wings by the end of the service. You come, anxious because of the silence in your life, and leave reassured by a clear word. God has been serving you. You come to serve God so that God might have a better opportunity to serve you. And I hope it will be a good show.

Which brings us to today's epistle from the book of Revelation. Friends, do you suffer from the post-Easter blahs? Has the ecstasy gone out of your Easter? Oh, it was great here two weeks ago. But now, on the eve of exams, and after Dallas, it's back to business as usual. And what difference did Easter make? Well, here's a song for the post-Easter doldrums.

> Then I looked, and I heard the voice of many angels surrounding the throne and the living creatures and the elders; they numbered myriads of myriads and thousands of thousands, singing with full voice,
>
> > "Worthy is the Lamb that was slaughtered
> > to receive power and wealth and wisdom and might
> > and honor and glory and blessing!"
>
> Then I heard every creature in heaven and on earth and under the earth and in the sea, and all that is in them, singing,
>
> > "To the one seated on the throne and to the Lamb
> > be blessing and honor and glory and might
> > forever and ever!"
>
> And the four living creatures said, "Amen!" And the elders fell down and worshiped.
>
> Revelation 5:11–14

This vision was addressed to a dispirited, disheartened church. The Easter exhilaration was past. There were persecutions by the emperor for some of these churches. Others were simply ignored by their pagan neighbors. Now, it was the long haul. This vision was given to John who was on the island of Patmos, the Alcatraz of the

Roman world. Was the whole Easter thing an idle tale? A dream? Wishful thinking?

What does God do for the post-Easter blahs? *God gives a vision, a show.*

The show opens when the curtain is raised in heaven itself (4:1). First we see the heavenly throne, surrounded by twenty-four elders seated upon their thrones (4:4). And what theatrical effects! There are flashes of lightning, peals of thunder. These announce that God himself is now on stage—heaven and earth quiver and shake before God.

Encircling the throne are four living creatures—a lion, a bull, a human, an eagle—who shout unceasing praise to God on the throne and sing as the elders bow in unison.

Next, the spotlight falls upon a scroll sealed with seven seals. A book so well-sealed must contain the deepest of mysteries. But no one in the heavenly court can break the seals. Then, from the misty backstage there emerges a Lamb whose bloody wounds show that it has been slaughtered. As it moves center stage, the whole heavenly court becomes a great choir singing homage to the Lamb, homage that they previously gave only to God. Hallelujah! The Lamb is worthy to break the seals (5:9–10), his wounds make him worthy.

And it is here that today's text, Revelation 5, begins. The chorus, bigger than even our chapel choir, widens to include voices of thousands of angels, animals, elders, all circling the throne, moving in concentric processional, all moving, singing, looking to the throne. "Praise to the Lamb!" they sing, "Power, wealth, wisdom, might, honor, glory, blessing" (5:12)—you've heard our choir do it at the *Messiah*, just like that.

The circle widens even further to include not only the elders, the four animals, the angelic hosts, but every single living creature "in heaven and on earth and under the earth and in the sea" (5:13). There is no corner of creation where some creature, some beetle or goldfinch or blue whale, is not singing for all its worth.

The anthem now heaps every accolade on the Lamb that can be sung: "power, wealth, wisdom, might, honor, glory and blessing" (5:12). The chorus prepares us for the breaking of the seals and the scene ends with the Lamb and God, seated together, center stage backed by a loud, operatic, "Amen."

O what a lovely show!

And what does it mean? What does a wild vision like that mean for ordinary people like you and me? What difference does it make that the slaughtered Lamb sits beside exalted God, the Creator almighty, on the golden throne at the center of heaven?

A friend of mine, Jim Wallis of the Sojourners Community in Washington, was visiting Coretta Scott King during the celebration of the birthday of Martin Luther King, Jr. She asked him to go to the Georgia State Penitentiary and visit a young man who has been in jail since he was sixteen and murdered a young woman. He has been on death row for three years. He will be executed later this year. Wallis said that, when he saw him, the first thing that the young man said was, "Hey preacher, what's the good news?"

"For one long moment," Wallis said, "I looked at this one who would be dead in a few months for having caused the death of another and I didn't know any good news."

Two weeks ago, when the glorious Easter services here were done and the show was over, I went to my office to disrobe and there was a note on my desk. The note said, "We are from South Carolina and were in the chapel this morning because our twelve-year-old son is in Duke Hospital, paralyzed. Thanks for the beautiful service." Does a beautiful show explain a paralyzed twelve-year-old boy? What difference does it make?

Well, what word do you say to the victims of those on death row and to those who are on death row? What is the good news for a paralyzed child and his parents? If there is a word it must be bigger, grander, than our usual prosaic exhortations for self-help. It will have to be a word that's cosmic, poetic, outside, beyond the bounds of the expected, the conventional. It will be sung by a choir rather than argued by a preacher—that sort of word.

The Lamb, who a few weeks ago was stripped, beaten, humiliated, and nailed on a cross to die, this one now sits enthroned in glory next to the Creator of the universe. Everything that God has—all wisdom, power, blessing, and honor—now belongs to the Lamb, the Lamb who knows what it's like to be on death row because he's been there, the Lamb who knows what it's like to be helpless because he's been there. And because the Lamb, who has been here, sits on the throne up there, we do have something to show the child dying of starvation in the African desert, the refugee perishing in the camp in Lebanon, the young man on death row in Atlanta, the child in Duke Hospital. What we show is a vision of a new heaven and a new earth where the one who was slain, in behalf of all these who are slain, now rules in glory. O gentle, hurting, baffled, tearful ones, wherever you languish within the sound of my voice, peer through the bars of your cell, turn your head to catch the light through your hospital window, see the vision and hear the song, sung by hosts in heaven and choirs on earth, "Worthy is the Lamb that was slaughtered!"

Now That's a Horse of a Different Color!

Amanda J. Burr

During a welcome respite from their arduous journey along the yellow brick road and across the field of poppies, Dorothy and Toto, the Scarecrow, the Tin Woodsman, and the Lion, are chauffered about in a coach drawn by a magical, mystifying, lusciously colorful horse. As they ride around and around the Emerald City's fountain in the square, the horse changes color from emerald green to royal purple, glorious yellow, and brilliant orange, right in front of their delighted eyes. When the riders ask the coachman—whom we know to be the wizard in disguise—what kind of horse it is, he chortles and answers: "Why, that's the horse of a different color." The laughter and singing that follow, with a "Hah-Hah-Hah" and a "Ho-Ho-Ho" and a couple of "La-Dee-Dahs," is how they passed the day away in the merry old land of Oz.

John of Patmos gives some indication of how the Christ-followers passed the latter days of the first century away in the not-so-merry land of the Roman Empire. His book of Revelation is filled with images of lions and lambs and beasts with human features, along with horses of different hues. John's four horses in chapter 6 are not beasts of burden, or perhaps they are. Because each one carries on its back a messenger of doom. The horse and rider alike are of the same hue, perhaps calling to our minds pictures of the black or white or silver armor-clad Arthurian knights. But these are

---

Amanda J. Burr is pastor of the First Christian Church of Reseda, California.

not a welcome sight in the mind's eye of John's readers. They are the four horses and horsemen of the Apocalypse, who gallop from the future back through time to purge the present from the past.

Although John saw the horses and horsemen arriving at any moment in his time, we try to figure out when they will come in our time, as if they had not yet arrived. I believe the truth to be that they have already been here, they are here now, and they are coming again. The four horsemen of the Apocalypse ride among us, confronting us every day of the world. Thus is this text relevant for today, not as a book of secret prophecies that can only be decoded by a select group of alarmist paranoids, but as a constant reminder that the Divine is attentive to what we do and how we are with one another. John's wondrous images hold within them timeless significance to awaken and arouse even the sleepiest Christian and the most arrogant humans—with ears, that is, to hear. So let us leap headlong and unafraid into the middle of this scene.

Not the Long Ranger, Red Rider, Cisco Kid, Hopalong Cassidy, or even Zorro—these four are not heroes by any stretch of the imagination. Each horse of a different hue and each rider is trouble for any and all who are found in their path. The colors are sickly, impure, even putrid—not technicolor or bright. The white is not radiant; the red is not scarlet; the black is neither crisp nor soft; and the pale is not pastel, but pasty.

For John's readers, the White horse and archer conjured up images of the dread Parthians, "who were the only mounted archers of the first century. White horses were their trademark."[1] The White horse gallops today, bearing the archer upon its back. He is the announcer and the dreaded first strike of a divinely engineered war. He and his companions are on a mission to create turmoil and havoc. They are to rout the wicked. Red is the color of slaughter, Black is the color of famine. Pale is the color of death. It is as if each horse and horseman symbolize the stages of a war and its aftermath. First the conquest and slaughter of the vanquished, followed by a time of famine and plague amongst the living remnant and their eventual demise as the victims of the war. The evidence of these trampling hooves is strewn throughout history.

We imagine the conquering White horseman wielding a weapon of destruction, likening the archer's bow and arrows to our own familiar weapons of war, our long-range heat-seeking missiles of mega-death and destruction. But the bow and arrow are subtler weapons that must be aimed meticulously at their prey. It is not a noisy weapon, but the flight of the arrow is straight and sure in the hands of an expert archer. We suppose we would hear the noisy gallop of the conqueror, but the White horse is a stealthy pacer, prancing through our self-righteous, imperious midst. It is not with bombs and rifles and automatic weapons that the White horseman shall conquer us. But subtly, silently, step by stealthy step, the conqueror shall wage his war. His arrows are soaked with the poison of greed and thoughtlessness, so that his victims will sell their heritage, their land, their neighbor, even their souls, for a few coins. The war has begun and the White horse rides through the hallowed corridors of Wall Street and the computer bytes that conduct sterile corporate warfare with surprise takeovers. No one can hear him, for his horse's hooves are covered with animal skins and his arrow is swift-piercing, clean through the heart.

Next the Red horse and rider gallop forth as they are called. What does the color red symbolize in your mind's eye? Go with the most obvious. Blood, passion, turmoil. The red stripes on our nation's flag symbolize the blood shed in war, the blood of the martyrs of a war launched by humans upon humans. The Red horse rides through time and is permitted—and the author means permitted by Almighty God—to take away peace from the earth so that humans should slay one another.

When we are in the path of the Red horse, we are trampled under its hooves. The Red horse is the "source of war and combats, provoking scourges and catastrophes."[2] When war breaks out, there are lots of human reasons for it, but there is also "the decision of the red horse, the spirit of war...in the heart of history."[3] I think the Red rider is permitted to take away peace not only from the earth but from the individual human soul as well. The political machinery of a nation gears up for war by spending money on its war weapons and sapping the resources of its people. Peace is removed as the Red rider gallops through the judgment of those who would siphon monies away from health care and mental health care, housing for the poor, and education programs for the children. Peace is removed as the Red rider gallops through the federal courts where decisions are made to remove people's freedoms. Peace is removed as the Red rider gallops into a society where the victims of crimes are treated with less respect, compassion, and fairness than the perpetrators of crimes. The Red rider gallops in and out of our lives at every moment of frustrated rage, turmoil, or conflict. The Red rider is galloping in the moments when we wage personal war upon another in an attempt to assert our own will upon others, even in our own families. The Red rider is part and parcel of the everyday fracases, battles, and tribulations that disrupt and take peace from human relationships.

The Black horse is called forth next. What does the color black symbolize in your mind's eye? Go with the most obvious. Darkness, blindness or being unable to see, fear of being lost, mourning. The horseman mounted on the Black horse carries not a sword but a balance in his hand—a scale of weights and measures like that held in the hand of the blindfolded Ms. Justice. And the voice of John's creature announces: "A quart of wheat for a day's pay, and three quarts of barley for a day's pay." One quart of wheat or three quarts of barley will cost dearly. The Black horse is the herald of famine, often a consequence of war.[4] But famine is also a consequence of inflated prices and greed based on the laws of supply and demand. The greater the demand, the higher the price. The Black horse rides through human history everyday and his rider threatens the lives of the poor and the oppressed and the distressed. The Black horse trots through the streets of our hometown and has settled on the door-steps of our neighbors. We are perhaps more terrified of the Black horse than we are of the Red horse, for there are no weapons other than love and self-sacrifice to tip the heavily weighted scales of greed.

The proclamation, "Do not damage the olive oil and the wine!" is an allusion to two luxuries. Do we not live in a time when farmers are paid not to produce foodstuffs, while human beings succumb to the weighted balances of the Black horse and rider everyday? Do we not see glimpses of his trail on our items of video luxury, while we absent-mindedly consume full quarts of wheat and barley? Upon the balances of the horseman are weighted food and money. The message is: a little food costs a lot of money. Luxuries are plentiful, but essentials are in demand. The Black horse trumpets the power of money. With money we can get what we need. We can also get what we do not need. The Black horse breeds greed and represents the power of the economy and a particular economic system. As strange as it sounds, it seems to me that the more money there is to be had, the greater is the greed for it. Money equals power. Where the Black horse treads, money means control; money means security; money means wealth, authority, and prestige; and in some folks' perverted, convoluted thinking, money means fulfillment. I say to you, the Black horse rides on the promise of a single lottery ticket or a roll of the dice.

Finally, the Pale horse is called forth, whose rider has a name: "Death." The rider has a companion who follows him and his name is "Hades." The pale horse is livid, sickly, anemic, ridden by the one called "Pestilence," "Disease," and "Death." The horseman and his companions are limited, given power over only one-fourth of the earth. They are *not* limited to striking down only the wicked of the earth. All of humanity is subject to their power. Pestilence and death ride over the earth in every moment of history and our brothers and sisters succumb to the sword that they wield everyday.

We have banded together to stand against the devastation of the Pale horse and rider, when Pestilence got too close to including us in his numbers. But we have ignored him when we thought that he was not anywhere near us. Now he rides through our streets at this very moment, choosing some of our number to afflict with a pestilence that has no cure. AIDS is the plague of the moment. Perhaps three-fourths of the earth have endured the plagues of syphilis, bubonic plague, red death, tuberculosis, typhoid, small-pox, diptheria, cholera, scarlet fever, measles, mumps, chicken pox, and even polio, but the Pale horseman still rides and AIDS is the sword he wields today. Thousands have been martyred by this horseman and yet we stand in his path as if beckoning him to strike us down. We pray that we shall be among the three-fourths of the earth that Pestilence and Hades cannot touch. But there is no such assurance.

History continues. Although the White, Red, Black, and Pale horses gallop at every moment, so too does the Word of God, whispered on the breath of the Holy Spirit, which breathes life into the faint of heart, breaks and converts the arrogant of will, and offers the soul peace in the midst of tribulation. A world that shall breathe in the Spirit of God and cleave to the truth shall withstand the onslaught of all the horses and riders through to the End.

But the End is *not* yet and, for now, we must recognize the horses and their riders when they are galloping in our midst. Perhaps it is not within our human power to conquer them or overthrow them. Perhaps it is only the King of kings and Lord of lords, the Christ crowned with light, the one called Faithful and True, who is equipped to do that. (See 19:11–16.) And yet this Christ has come among us: a conqueror of the past, the present, and the future. This Christ *in us* is our link with God. Keep your eyes upon him and when the White horse, the Red horse, the Black horse, and the Pale horse ride into your life, call them what they are. Say:

> I recognize you. I know your tricks and I know your plans
> and, no matter what you do or will for me or mine or the

world, there is another who will conquer you and yours in the End. . . !

And he rides the horse of a different color!

Amen.

Notes

[1]M. Eugene Boring, *Revelation* (Louisville: John Knox Press, 1989), pp. 118-124.

[2]Jacques Ellul, *Apocalypse* (New York: Seabury Press, 1977), p. 148.

[3]*Ibid.*

[4]*Ibid.*, p. 149.

OVERHEARING LOVE'S MUSIC IN A BRUTAL WORLD

Thomas H. Troeger

You are on a trip;
    and have just settled into a motor lodge for the night.
        The sign out front reads:
            "Free Cable Television in Every Room."

The people next door have already turned on their set.
    The words of the movie they are watching
        are only vaguely intelligible.

But you can tell from the soundtrack,
    It is a picture of romance and love,
        something to pull on the heartstrings.

You switch on your own television to the news network.
    There is no sound.
        You look at the screen anyway,
            hoping the sound will come on
                once the set warms up.

Thomas H. Troeger is professor of preaching at the Iliff School of Theology, Denver, Colorado.

Soldiers with semi-automatic rifles are leading four handcuffed men
    into a bare room with a plain table and a microphone.
From the television set on the other side of the wall
    you hear a surge of romantic music
        and the voices of the actors
            speaking passionately to each other.
You catch bits of phrases here and there:
    "…I promise you. . ."
    "…and no more shall we…"
    "…but only love…."
The voices fade.

All you hear is misty music.

Meanwhile,
    the handcuffed prisoners and their guards
        disappear from your silent screen.
            You see the newscaster
            followed by
                the next on-the scene report:
Seagulls and fish are covered with sticky black oil.
    People in raincoats are raking and shoveling the beach,
        which is also covered with the same viscous sludge.

        Ta ta ta taaaa!
        Ta ta ta taaaa!

You distinctly hear the sound of Mendelssohn's "Wedding March."
    The movie in the next room must be ending.
        The trumpets are making their famous triumphal call:

        Ta ta ta taaaa,
        Ta ta ta taaaa!

While you watch a shore worker
    pick up a large dead bird covered with oil,
    you imagine the grand wedding procession on the other set,
        the bride in white,
        the smiling groom.

The newscast images on your television insist on one reality
    while the music coming through the wall
        keeps awakening a different scene.

You hear someone in the next room click off the television.
    You watch in silence the face of the news announcer
        mouthing words you cannot hear.
            You decide the sound is never going to come on.
            You turn off the set and get ready for bed.

But you find a strange thing happening in your mind.
Usually when you click off the set,
    the images fade from consciousness.
        Then you begin to think about the day that is past
        and what faces you tomorrow.

But things are different tonight.

The images of the handcuffed people and the oil-covered creatures
    do not fade from your mind.
        You find they are held there by the love music
            that keeps replaying itself in your head.
The music that you thought was a sentimental intrusion
    upon the real world of the news show
        has done something that broadcast words
            have never accomplished.
The music has amplified the dissonance
    between the brutality of the world

and the hopes of the human heart for a life of
tenderness,
fidelity,
love.

Even if the movie was a Hollywood concoction,
there is no denying those yearnings of the heart
that it has stirred.
If you had heard the love music entirely on its own
or
If you had watched the news entirely on its own,
the effect would have been different.
Then you would have entered one reality or the other.
You would have accepted each on its own terms.
But now it is the juxtaposition
of the two worlds
that is haunting your imagination.
The contrast between the news images and the soundtrack
has broken the grip that the talk of the broadcasters
usually holds upon you.
Instead of concluding,
"That's the way the world is,"
you find yourself thinking:
"The world does not have to be that way.
The heart knows other possibilities."
As you go to bed and the music continues to echo in your memory,
you find yourself praying for those handcuffed people
whose names you did not even hear
and for those fish and birds suffocated in oil.

That moment of prayer
awakened by the music of love
brings you close to the spirit of John,
the writer of the book of Revelation.

Although he had no television,
> like you, he had an imagination
>> that filled with images
>>> and with the sound of remembered music.
Also like you, he knew the brutality of the world.
> The Roman authorities had exiled him to the island of Patmos
>> because of his Christian witness.
>> He was one of the more fortunate believers:
>> at least he had not been executed.
Nevertheless, exile is cruel and unusual punishment.
> There he was on a rocky island,
>> thirty-seven miles from the mainland,
>>> a man of passionate faith,
>>> now torn from the community
>>> whose worship and life had sustained him.

John looked out from the cliffs of Patmos,
> and the world appeared as violent to him
>> as it does to us when we watch the evening news.

He saw the Roman ships sailing by,
> soldiers and chariots crowded upon the decks.
>> But the soundtrack that played in his head
>>> was not the martial music of imperial Rome.
Instead,
> he heard the hymns of praise
>> that he remembered from the worship of his
>>> community.
Perhaps he forgot some of the words
or sometimes had difficulty recalling exactly how the tune went.
> But what he never forgot
>> was the music within the music,
>>> the assurance of faith
>>>> that the brutality of the world

                                        is not
                                the final
                                and triumphant
                                        reality of life.

The news from the mainland was bad.
        Christians needed shelter from persecution,
        they needed food and drink,
        they needed guidance when they were on the run,
        they needed comfort as they wept for those who had been
        slaughtered.
Thinking of these desperate people
        and imagining all of those who were yet to suffer
        before the kingdom of God was fully realized,
                John recalled a hymn,
                        or perhaps he composed it himself,
drawing inspiration from well-known verses
        out of the Psalms, Isaiah, and Ezekiel:

                Therefore are they before the throne of God,
                        [whom they] serve day and night within
                                [God's] holy temple;
                        and [God] who sits upon the throne
                                will shelter them with [God's own] presence.
                They shall hunger no more, neither thirst any more;
                        the sun shall not strike them,
                                nor any scorching heat.
                For the Lamb in the midst of the throne will be
                                their shepherd,
                        and he will guide them to springs of living water;
                and God will wipe away every tear from their eyes.
                                        (RSV, altered to be inclusive)

The music of that hymn,
    like the love music
        coming through the thin wall of the motor lodge
           stirred a vision in John
              that was utterly different
              from the Roman ships that passed
                before him.
His vision was a countervision to the vast worldly power
    that had exiled him
        and that was threatening the churches on the mainland.
John saw an alternative world,
    another reality,
    a different way of being.
And from that vision he drew strength for himself
    and for the churches he loved
    who were facing horrors they could not escape.
Like the music of love accompanying the news broadcast,
John's hymn is a reminder of the yearnings of the human heart.
And yet it is much more than that:
    the hymn is a declaration that
        the world
           will not always be
              the way
                the world
                  is now.

Look at the world before your eyes,
    but listen to John's hymn
        and let his vision rise in your heart.
Look at the battered women and children.
    "[God] who sits upon the throne

will shelter them with [God's own] presence."
Since God will shelter them,
we who claim God's name
will also provide shelter.
Look at the hollow eyes of a people needing bread.
"They shall hunger no more,
neither thirst any more."
Since God will feed them,
we who claim God's name
will also offer food.

Look at the people lost to drugs.
"For the Lamb in the midst of the throne
will be their shepherd,
and he will guide them
to springs of living water."
Since Christ will guide them,
we who claim to follow Christ
will point them to our savior.

Look at those who are mourning.
"God will wipe away every tear from their eyes."
Since God will comfort them,
we who claim God's name
will also give comfort.

Do not wait for the sound of the world
to go dead on your television
or to grow quiet in your head.
The world is intrusive and insistent.
Instead,
listen with John
and sing with John

until your song, your prayer, and your
action are one.
Then through your life others will hear John's hymn.
The world will lose its iron grip on their lives.
and they will be empowered
to sing and act in unison
with all those who declare:

"Blessing
and glory
and wisdom
and thanksgiving
and honor
and power
and might
be to our God for ever
and ever! Amen."
(7:12)

THIS BITTERSWEET SEASON

Ola Irene Harrison

Counseling junior camp one summer
I was confronted by the mystery
The beauty of this season now four weeks upon us

We were studying the liturgical year
Each day devoted to one season
And one thoughtful child asked why we use the same color
The color purple
For Lent as we do for Advent

My cocounselor and I tried to explain
The difference in the two seasons
(As if our explanations would help make any sense of it)
The child listened
And thought
Then said "But they're not the same. Let Advent be purple.
But Lent just feels
Gray."

Ola Irene "Cricket" Harrison, a minister of the Christian Church (Disciples of Christ), is a doctoral candidate at the School of Theology at Claremont, California.

Lent just feels gray

Those four words sum up for me my own uneasiness about Lent
These six weeks that follow Ash Wednesday
      are always uncomfortable for me
Forty-two days that I just want to rush through
To get to Easter

This time of silence
Of self-reflection
Of discipline and sacrifice is oppressive
Even dangerous

Lent makes me brace myself for something awful
But something wonderful at the same time
This season is bittersweet

Bittersweet

The very mention of the word makes my mouth water
My eyes smart
Never mind that my chocolate-lover friends assure me that
Bittersweet is the only kind of chocolate worth having

Never mind that my own memory (perhaps yours as well)
Holds most dear those moments of poignance
That strange combination of joy and pain

Bittersweet

Funny how just three syllables describe so vividly
The problem
(The meaning, perhaps?) of being
Human

Especially when called to be human before God
When challenged to be *faithful* before God

The writer of Revelation
Sets this challenge in a great drama
What a scene John describes!

A mighty angel from heaven
Wrapped in a cloud
A rainbow over his head
His face like the sun and
Legs like pillars of
Fire....

Just a little scroll and some bizarre instructions
For this scroll is not to be read
But to be eaten:
"Take it and eat it. It will be bitter to swallow,
        although in your mouth it will taste as sweet as honey."

The seer takes the scroll with its sweet taste
Swallows it
Immediately his stomach sours
Just as the angel had said

Yet he is given no time to recover
Not even time to suffer

No
He is told
That he will prophesy yet again
To many people, nations, and tongues
The message may sicken him
But it *is* the message he is called to preach

At this point
A voice inside me cries to stop the action
"Don't do this thing, John! Why open yourself to trouble like this?
	Why give yourself deliberately to the pain? Perhaps there
	are words best left unspoken, messages best left unheard.
	Why subject yourself to this?"

"Don't do this thing!"

Peter must have thought the question was justified
When he rebuked Jesus
He has just proclaimed his friend, his teacher as the
Messiah
God's anointed one
The hope of the living God

Only to have this one say he would be killed?
What kind of justice is that?
Jesus had to be mistaken
God would not allow
God's own messenger to die!

"God forbid that this happen to you."

And any sensible friend would have understood the loyalty
The love prompting that protest

but Jesus turns the rebuke upside down telling Peter
"Get out of my way, Satan, for your plane is a human plane.
Only God can fathom what it is God has in mind."
					(Matthew 16:13–25)

Peter knew well the sweet side of following his Lord
But the bitterness
The cost of following
Was only beginning to come clear

This one who first confessed
Would deny Jesus
This one who stridently insisted that
Jesus must not die
Would watch
helplessly
As that same Jesus would hang upon a cross

And I can't help but wonder
Is this why Lent is so difficult for me?
Because I see this Jesus walking a road
        that I fear to walk?
Because the costs of following Jesus
        to the cross are just too high?
Is this why I want to keep John from eating
His bittersweet scroll?

Lent is a season of hard questions
The hardest of all being "Why?"
Why does Jesus have to go to Jerusalem?
Why does John have to eat the scroll?
Why is God doing this?

These questions frame my own private torment
As a woman in ministry

It is a question I have heard expressed in many ways
By many of my sisters
Ordained and not ordained
Officially accepted by their denominations
Or castigated by their church leaders for seeking
        to follow their own religious sensibilities

"Why is God doing this (to me)?"

Why is it that I have been called to preach
        a message that may only be partly heard
(If acknowledged at all)?
Why did my seminary professors encourage me
        on my pilgrimage toward ordination
        when I cannot find a congregation
        that can pay a living wage?
How is it that judicatory leaders verbally embrace
        women in ministry
But I hold in my file a letter saying
        "Yes, they felt you were better qualified,
        But they believe the pastor really should be a man"?
John's sweet but bitter scroll
Is common food for many in ministry
(And not only women)
But for all those who have been called to speak
A difficult word on behalf of Jesus Christ
All pastors who struggle to speak both the comfort
        and the challenge of the gospel
All those who champion causes that conflict with
        "the way things have always been"
Called to preach for the sake of
Christ's church and for the sake of God's creation
Not only ministers but all Christians seeking to witness
        to God's presence in this world
Speaking hope when there is no hope
        peace when there is no peace
        light when all you can see is utter darkness

How long we stood at the nursery window I cannot say
The new grandmother anxiously watching
        her premature grandson
Fight for life in the incubator
While upstairs his mother was dying

Comatose
Terminal cancer
The growth had eaten through the spinal covering
    and was blocking the nerve impulses
      at the base of the brain
Nerve signals that governed basic life functions
Inoperable

The stricken grandmother had argued
    time and time again with her daughter
About ending the pregnancy
Buying some small bit of time
By not adding the physical stress of an unborn child
(All of that before the disease began
to spread so quickly)

Now she stood
Caught between willing her grandson to live
And allowing her daughter to die
With every hard question of life shining in her eyes
She looked at me and cried
"Why would God do this?"

But before I could bring myself to answer
She answered herself
And her new answer—
A new question—
Offered the only possible hope:
"How will I get through this, if not for God's help?"

The answering question to all our cries:
    "Don't do this thing, John!"

"God forbid that this happen to you!"
"Why is God doing this to us?"
Rises before us

We see a prophet eating the word of God
And fighting his rising gorge
At the words he is compelled to speak

We struggle to keep focus
Through all the suffering:
    Jesus
    Peter
    John
    Others
    Ourselves

But the truth also rises
Even with its bitterness the little scroll the seer ate
Signified no less than the presence of God
The sweet and beautiful presence of God

God help you Jesus
God help you Peter
God help you John
God help you sisters in ministry
God help us all

And in these gray and often bitter Lenten days
May God grant us strength
And courage to seek the sweetness of God's presence

How else can we hope to live faithfully
If not for God's help?

Amen

PROPHETS VERSUS THE BEASTS

John M. Lurvey, Jr.

The strapping, balding, golden-haired man in tights is Hulk Hogan. He fills Madison Square Garden and sets records on the cable network. "The Hulkster" as he calls himself is a chief among an army of neck-twisters and bone-benders of wrestlemania. These roly-poly warriors act out, in a mixture of ritual and hype, the epic battles that mirror the great myths of the ages. Here good and evil battle with all ambiguities removed. A wide consensus of literary analysts, anthropologists, and biblical scholars find the hero-conflict story to be a living symbol that shapes the understanding of life in many cultures. The story of the hero's triumph is told and retold in a million, million stories. It is a story that particularly stirs young males I've met in male consciousness groups. Many guys yearn for a time when a man could feel good by using skill and violence in the role of being a rescuer, protector, and hunter.

Unfortunately, the male protector and hunter can be corrupted. Instead of being a noble knight he becomes the ignoble exploiter of oppressed people and polluter of the planet. Yet the hero/heroine story has a universal appeal for us.

In today's readings from the Revelation of John 11:1–13 and 13:1–18, we have a retelling of the hero story. The whole book of Revelation is an "unveiling" or Apocalypse of the actual meaning of life itself. John, the visionary, casts the whole life story in the setting

---

John M. Lurvey, Jr. is pastor of the Normal Heights United Methodist Church, San Diego, California.

of a great cosmic war between the Almighty Creator and the unequal but dangerous Dragon-Adversary.

The heavenly court is represented by its champion, the fatally wounded Lamb, who ends up winning in the end and taking the Bride. Before this usual ending of the hero drama, there are strange and important twists on this telling of the hero story. Chapter 12, midway in the drama of Revelation, records the birth of the Hero and the introduction of the Dragon-Adversary. On each side of this center are two pair of adversaries that I invite you to consider. Chapter 11 introduces two prophets. These two righteous "lampstands" and "olive trees" possess the powers of Elijah, Elisha, and Moses combined. They call down fire, plague, and drought on any who oppose them. The two prophets use fear and force to subdue the human race to conform to their exhortations. It should not surprise us that these two prophets are not liked by the people of the earth. They represent holy coercion such as that advocated by some of today's Christian reconstructionists and their ancestors. There lurks in the shadow of some moralists the false optimism that mere violence and fear can create public righteousness and reform perversion.

Now on the far side of the center of the Apocalypse drama two beasts are introduced in chapter 13. One beast is from the sea and the other is from the land. One of the beasts later becomes known as the "false prophet." The symbolism of the first beast is a mixture of heads, governing authority, and animal-like qualities. Like the Lamb-Hero of Revelation, one of its heads seems to be mortally wounded and yet it now lives. The ten-horned, seven-headed, lion-mouthed, bear-footed beast draws its power from the great Dragon-Adversary. The Dragon uses words of slander and blasphemy uttered through the beast to attack God and the people identified with God.

The other beast has two horns like the Lamb-Hero but speaks like the Dragon-Adversary. This beast can match the prophets' ability to call down fire from heaven. The beastly signs and wonders inspire people to worship the first beast whose mortal wound is healed. This second beast makes even the image of the first beast appear to live and speak. The people of the world are attracted to the beasts and receive the number symbol of the beast on their hand or forehead.

God's Dilemma

In their confrontation, these two beasts kill the two prophets. The people of the earth celebrate the prophets' death. These two pairs, prophets and beasts, represent an element in God's dilemma.

God can choose to act through righteous dictators that force conformity, but that does not inspire genuine devotion and love. Resentment and resistance are the results.

This hero story has further twists. First, Evil with a capital *E* seems to have a reflective, almost imitative quality. When God acts through the slain Lamb or two prophetic witnesses with fiery power, Evil acts in a similar fashion—only more so. Second, the struggle between God and Evil in the story is woven tightly within the warp and woof of the human life of the creation that God loves and called good. Like Jesus' parable of the darnel planted among the good grain, God faces an awesome choice. God can either eradicate Evil and lose the creation or continue the creation and accept the presence of Evil. The Revelation story tells us God can do one or the other but not both. Third, this hero story "reveals" the surprising nearness of our own heroic significance.

Our Choice

The prophet John's late, great revision of the hero story now reveals to each of us the true nature of our choice and God's dilemma. Archibald MacLeish in his play, *J. B.*, tries to dramatize the vision of God's dilemma. He saw the problem this way—if God is good, then he/she is not almighty and if God is almighty, then she/he is not good. God in Revelation has both power and love. God must choose. God does choose. God has chosen to delay the display of power against the already defeated Dragon-Adversary in order to love and continue the creation. God's choice of love is an awesome one. It is costly. It costs the world full of centuries of the long oppression of the poor, women, and colorful people. It costs holocausts and wars. It costs the personal tragedies of earthquakes in great cities and hurricanes on tropical paradise islands. It costs each of us who face the risk of a traffic accident in our routine commute or painful death by cancer because of too much lead or asbestos at our job site. In these moments of tragedy and acute personal and collective pain, it feels like too much of a price. We cry out to the stars, like Albert Camus, and vent our rage against the God we don't believe in any more.

"Helen" felt like that as she lay on her hospital pillow. She was frightened and angry at her recently discovered condition. A neurological malformation could, with the slightest alteration, turn her into "a mindless vegetable." Bitterly she wept to herself, "Why me? Why me?" Then, in the awesome silence of her inner dialogue, came another voice that intervened with the question "Why not you?"

"Why am I so special that I am spared the dilemmas of life's risks?" she pondered. Out of the fierce quiet of that inner dialogue Helen experienced a renewal of faith. She became grateful to her Creator for each day of wholeness that she received rather than desperately angry over the future that could no longer be taken for granted.

Our choice is our attitude toward God's choice to continue creation. For God to lovingly choose not to be the all-controlling dictator and the all-consuming victor over Evil in all its forms implicates each of us in these painful decisions. We can bitterly reject God like the angry adolescent who demands that all of life be fair. Revelation's alternative is to choose to affirm, celebrate, and even dance to the rhythms of failure like Zorba the Greek. My friend Howard says that each day he can choose the way of self-pity, which leads to self-victimization, or the way of celebration, which leads to recovery. Howard's alcoholism can be interpreted by himself as a curse that robs him of a lifestyle that others can enjoy, or it is God's special blessing that spares him the self-deceptions and drifting inauthenticity lived by so many. Howard's choice makes all the difference between his sanity and self-destruction.

That is why John retells that hero story with all its bloody, bizarre boldness. He is trying to reveal to us a truth that philosophical argument or mathematical formula can not bring to expression. The episode of the prophets and the beasts leads us into the vicarious experience of story time. We are exposed to the reality of God's dilemma of love and power and our choice of a response. As John the prophet and "Helen" and "Howard" reveal, it makes all the difference.

Our Significance

Finally, the battle between the prophets and the beasts unveils to us a new significance for our life in the great urban anthills or peasant villages we reside in today. Our individual feelings of insignificance breed apathy and quiet futility that erupt in the actions of a Bernard Goetz who tries to save himself by shooting at whatever threatens him in his oppressive world. Revelation and its battles put the reader into a mighty cosmic conflict in which everyone can be a hero or heroine right where they are. The Apocalypse of John reveals that we are nearer than we think to significance and even everlasting greatness. Our weapons are not produced by Smith and Wesson but from suffering, struggle, patience, and persistence that is sweetened by the presence of God's Holy Spirit of assurance. Our weapons are the new self and new community God calls us to become. This is not insignificant. It connects our life story to the central story of the universe.

Carl C. Williams writes that a German schoolteacher named Reis had nearly developed a telephone before Alexander Graham Bell. The Reis invention could carry sounds over distance but could not turn them into voice reproductions. Later Mr. Bell replicated the Reis invention and found his mistake. By tightening a small screw by a tiny fraction of an centimeter the Reis invention could have become the first telephone. Germany's Herr Reis was just slightly short of being a great hero and pioneer of the telephone. Likewise, Revelation involves each of us in the call for heroism in the Great Cosmic Struggle very near to each of us.

John the prophet spoke to lukewarm third-generation Christians who were accommodating to their Hellenistic culture. He bore a call from heaven to reclaim the Christian vocation of heroic obedience and unseasonable faithfulness to the spirit of the New Age. He sought to awaken and enlighten village and urban Asian Christians into the true road of greatness. He challenged them and he still challenges us to respond to the Christian calling to a heroic life right where we are: in the packing houses, classrooms, computer terminals, restaurants, and apartments where we all live and move and respond to the challenge to become new beings together. If we take this truth seriously, we do not require the escapist fantasy of Hulk Hogan. To be a Christian is not merely to wrestle against flesh and blood people but "against the rulers, against the authorities, against the cosmic powers of this present darkness, against the spiritual forces of evil in the heavenly places" (Ephesians 6:12).

WITHIN REACH OF THE DRAGON

Peter Vaught

The Bible verses I read talk about the woman and child being threatened and chased by that terrible red dragon. The image of that scene would be enough to terrify any child going to bed in a dark room. All alone. These verses describe people in trouble: people facing a force they could not defeat or outrun. I believe, as many scholars now believe, the heart of this revelation is of Jewish origin, later edited by Christians as a word of hope in the face of Rome's persecution of their struggling churches.

The dragon was going to devour the woman's child. Most of us accept that women are easy marks of prey. Most of us understand that children are easy targets for people who want to harm them. My dad was an easy mark and target too. The force of evil beat at our door.

My family did not believe in myths, unless you want to include superstitions. They would not put a hat on a bed. They would not rock a rocking chair with no one in it. No, my family did not believe in myths but they lived them. My mom and dad lived out one of the oldest myths people know about: the threat that our carefully crafted lives would be destroyed. My parents, my sister, and I did our best to live with the threat of having our lives fall apart. We tried to portray the picture of the typical family: dad, mom, a boy, and a girl, the normal American family. But the dragon was wait-

---

Peter Vaught is pastor of the Griffith United Methodist Church, Las Vegas, Nevada.

ing to devour us all. This was the force in my family that worked to tear us apart, bring us unhappiness, and wreck our hope that we belonged together. I know what the force was that threatened us. It reached like claws into our family to tear us apart from one another. It was not Satan. It was the terrible force of evil that he has come to represent.

Usually, we think of dads as being strong and protective. I believed that lie for a long time. Eventually, I discovered that my dad was as weak as everyone else. We were within reach of the dragon.

It is a dim memory. But I can still see the colors. I can still feel my guts stirred up. My mom and I are sitting in a car and it is getting dark. The car is parked by a building. On either side of the door into the building there is a row of glass bricks. The light from inside the building plays funny tricks as it comes through the glass bricks—red, green, blue— and it is almost as if it is Christmas. But it is not. There is a man talking to my mother. He is telling her that he told my dad we were outside waiting. I remember…that it was a bar. I do not remember my dad coming out.

My family looked at the world from a strange point of view. They thought of themselves as if they were simply leaves before the wind. You have seen the wind blow leaves; leaves cannot seem to do anything about the force that pushes them along. I guess that is why my mother married three alcoholics, my dad being the second on the list. I guess that is why my father would run from relationships. He left his first wife for a neighbor woman several times. He left my mother several times. Mom never said that he left for another woman. I think she was just protecting her fragile fantasy. Maybe she thought she was protecting me. The idea of her protecting me does not seem to fit. The force of evil was at work, trying with all its power to destroy the fabric of our family. We were within reach of the dragon.

It is a vivid memory. It was Friday afternoon and we were going to a spaghetti dinner someplace in town. It was a year or so after my father died. I was eleven years old. We had walked out of the door and I confidently told my mom that I had the keys. So, I reared back and slammed the door. I can still remember as it slammed shut. My mom was over by the car with her purse open. It did not take her long to realize that neither she, nor I, had the keys. We were locked out. I went to the window by the back door. I did not mean to break it, but I did. My mother started whipping me for breaking her window. Did she whip me because of her frustration? That might have been part of it, but it was not all of it. The rest of that evening and all through Saturday she was out of control. She would whip me every time she thought of the broken window. I guess I could have taken the whipping. Most of us do at some time in our lives. I could not stand her words; her awful words ring in my ears now. With each barrage of blows she would tell me that she wished I had never been born. What a terrible thing to tell a child.

We remember things like this out of our past. Why did we not do something about it? Some kids do when they are facing emotional, physical, and sexual abuse. Many children take to the street, take refuge in the homes of families in the next state, or turn off the pain with anything they can get a hold of. I wonder sometimes why I did not run away.

I did not run away because, as crazy as it was, I needed the eggs. I desperately needed love. Who does not need love? I was willing to pay any price for the love. I would even be the target for Mom's angry blows and words because I would do anything to be loved. My sister would do anything as well. The red dragon was there. We were within reach of the dragon.

My sister was about fifteen the year before my father died. He was ill and had not gone to work for several months. My dad would get mad at one of us. He would refuse to talk for several days. Then there would be a big fight and everyone would say they were sorry. While Dad was sick he started getting mad at my sister. She did crazy things. But his pattern changed. He would get mad at my sister, not talk to her for several days, and then he would apologize to my sister and ask for her forgiveness.

That was strange enough, but then he started getting down on his knees and burying his face in her bosom. I can still see my sister looking at me from across the room, my father's face between her breasts. She had the same expression on her face that I imagine on the face of a cornered, helpless animal. He would cry and tell her he was sorry. But that was not what it looked like to me. What I saw could have been titled, "What's wrong with this picture?" It was supposed to be normal. I remember thinking to myself, "Oh Dad, Dad, what you are doing is so wrong." It was about that time that my sister went to live with our older brother.

My family did not work because my mom and dad could not make themselves emotionally available to my sister and me. My father's drinking, desertion, and sexual abuse of my sister made it impossible for him to let anyone in. My mother's emotional dependence on my father, her unwillingness to rescue her daughter (because of the threat it posed to my dad's love), and her inability and unwillingness to control her anger all made her emotionally unavailable to her children.

I believe Mom and Dad loved us as best they could. I think they were incapable of loving us the way we needed to be loved because they were sick. Emotionally? I think that would be the easy answer: many seek counseling for emotional hurts and then restore their families to work the way they are supposed to. No. That was not going to work for us. It was deeper. It was their illness, but their illness made it the whole family's illness. We all suffered. Counseling does a lot of good and it probably could have helped my parents, but their illness was spiritual. We call this sin! Spiritual illness requires divine healing.

You might think you have escaped the chaotic life that my family lived. Maybe you did. If you did you are very fortunate. Statistics tell us that 94 percent of the people in our country come from families that did not function the way they were supposed to. Either Mom or Dad (sometimes both) were not emotionally there for the kids. The reasons one or both parents would not be in the home, nurturing the child, might include: hospitalization for physical or mental illness; alcoholism and substance abuse; compulsive gambling; emotional, sexual, and physical abuse; or desertion.

My family was blue-collar. You may think that because you came from a family in a higher socio-economic bracket you did not face the same risk. I have heard that 70 percent of the ministers in our country come from dysfunctional families. But, you may have been lucky and the statistics may have been with you. I will tell you this: I hope you were lucky. I hope you were blessed in such a way that you did not have to struggle against one of the most frightening faces of evil in our land.

I wanted to have a family like "Father Knows Best." I wanted a family where Mom and Dad really did know best: a family where my parents were strong and wise. I wanted a family where parents were noble in their words and actions. I did not think that it was too much to ask. I still do not think it was too much to ask. I hope you came from a family where Mom and Dad did look out for you. I hope you came from a family where you were cared for and loved and protected. If you did, you were lucky.

Most of the people I will come into contact with in my life were not so lucky. One of the most ugly faces of this mess is that most of the people I meet—people who have been raised in homes that did not work the way they were supposed to—have the biggest chance of doing the very same thing all over again to the people they love. Friends, the red dragon is a frightening face of evil.

Both of my parents are dead now. I received an inheritance from them. I have inherited feelings of being responsible for everything that happens. I have inherited not trusting my feelings. I have inherited not trusting others. This is the legacy my parents have given me. My mom and dad were not evil. They were weak like the rest of us. They were misinformed about many things. Like the rest of us. The dragon was there knocking at our door.

People from the beginning of time have fought this red dragon. The evil it represents has shown itself to be war, torture, persecution, political upheaval, abuse, and destruction. The dragon has broken the backs of nations, tribes, and families. At some point we lose sight of whether the dragon is reaching for us or whether we are reaching for the dragon. When we reach out to embrace the dragon we begin to perpetuate the destructive evil.

How do we get out of this mess? We cannot defeat or outrun the dragon on our own power. The first step is to honestly face the fact that our families are not the fantasies we hoped for. We must realize that there are literally hundreds of millions of people living a life of hurt and distrust. We start by refusing to lie and cover up. We find someone to talk with, maybe even a group who will listen. But this is only a part of the healing. In order for real healing of this spiritual illness to begin, we must let God bring love from the future to heal the past.

God has a plan. We may not be able to control the red dragon, but the power of God's love can not only control the dragon but defeat the dragon. Remember the Bible verses I read? The red dragon was ready to devour the child as the woman gave birth. The dragon wanted to destroy them both. God had something else in mind. God saved the child and the woman from destruction. God saved the innocent and the vulnerable from suffering. God can save us from that same destruction. We must honestly face our lifetime of hurt and let God begin the healing.

I went to counseling for several years. I knew something was wrong but I did not know what it was. I only knew that I was hurting inside. In the middle of the counseling, God gave me a dream.

I was ten, just before my dad died—ten years old with the biggest feet in the world. It was not easy navigating through a group of people with those big feet. During those last few weeks of my father's life, his ankles were painfully swollen. Whenever he bumped his ankles, pain shot through his body. I can remember walking through a room of visiting relatives. If I came close to him my father would caution: "Look out, Peter. Please don't bump into my ankles."

Seventeen years after my father's death, God gave me a dream. I dreamed my dad, my family, and I were on an uncle's farm. There was a circle of relatives sitting with my father. I was trying to get into the circle to see my dad. My father spoke as he saw me coming between the chairs, "Peter, watch out for my ankles." Hurt and rejected, I began to back away. As I did, the family members closed the gap and shut me out. Then, I heard my dad's voice saying, "Wait, Peter! Come here." I walked through the crowd of relatives. My dad put his arms around me. "I just want you to know," he said, "that I really love you."

With this dream of reconciliation and peace, God brought this child out of the reach of the red dragon.

📖 12:1–6, 13–17

WINGS OF EAGLES AND
HOLES IN THE EARTH

Marie M. Fortune

Spirit of the Living God, fall afresh on us. Open our ears and eyes, our hearts and minds. Prepare us to hear the truth before us, the truth that makes us flinch before it sets us free. Sit close by us this morning as we continue in our worship together. Amen.

Three days before Christmas, Delia Alaniz, thirty-six, was sentenced to ten years in prison by Judge Harry Follman in Skagit County Superior Court. She had pleaded guilty to second degree murder for hiring a hit man to kill her husband who had physically and sexually abused her for seventeen years. He had also beaten and molested their four children, ages eight to sixteen, for years. He threatened to go to their daughter instead. He threatened to rape her daughter in front of her; he held a gun to the children's heads demanding that they tell him who their mother's lover was; he beat them with a whip. Terrorized for most of their lives, the children's nightmares are now about their father coming back and raping their sister.

During the years of her abuse, Alaniz had gone to a shelter in Bellingham; she had had her husband arrested only to see him released the next day; she had escaped to her sister's house only to have him physically threaten other family members; she had taken

Marie M. Fortune is executive director of the Center for the Prevention of Sexual and Domestic Violence, Seattle, Washington.

out a protection order on him and he beat her for it; she had come to Seattle in 1987 only to be turned away from a shelter because she had her fifteen-year-old son with her; she had her sister move into her house to protect her but her husband's violence continued; she separated from him and tried to live alone but he would not let her go and kept her under surveillance. She was terrified of him and she knew there was no place else to go where she and her children could be safe. In desperation, she stopped his violence by having him killed. She is now serving her ten-year sentence in maximum security at Purdy Correctional Center.[1]

If ever there was a woman who knows deep inside what Psalm 55 is talking about, it is Delia Alaniz. Put yourself in her place for a moment and listen to these words:

> Give ear to my prayer, O God;
>   do not hide yourself from my supplication.
> Attend to me, and answer me;
>   I am troubled in my complaint....
> My heart is in anguish within me,
>   the terrors of death have fallen upon me.
> Fear and trembling come upon me,
>   and horror overwhelms me.
> And I say, "O that I had wings like a dove!
>   I would fly away and be at rest;
> truly, I would flee far away;
>   I would lodge in the wilderness;
> I would hurry to find a shelter for myself
>   from the raging wind and tempest."
>   Psalm 55:1–2a, 4–8

This was the terror that Delia knew for seventeen years. This was the terror that the children knew.

In Psalm 22, we also hear this fear described:

> I am poured out like water,
>   and all my bones are out of joint;
> my heart is like wax;
>   it is melted within my breast;
> my mouth is dried up like a potsherd,
>   and my tongue sticks to my jaws;
>   you lay me in the dust of death.
>
>   Psalm 22:14–15

The psalmist knew how it feels to be terrorized.

And the psalmist also knew how it feels to be terrorized by someone very, very close, as did Delia:

> It is not enemies who taunt me—
> I could bear that;
> it is not adversaries who deal insolently with me—
> I could hide from them.
> But it is you, my equal,
> my companion, my familiar friend,
> with whom I kept pleasant company;
> we walked in the house of God with the throng.
> Psalm 55:12–14

It was not an enemy; it was her husband, the father of her children. One might expect this assaultive behavior from a stranger or an adversary, but one does not expect and should not expect such things from the one to whom one is joined in the covenant of marriage.

Then the psalmist goes on and offers a promise:

> But I call upon God
> and the LORD will save me....
> Evening and morning and at noon
> I utter my complaint and moan,
> and [God] will hear my voice.
> [God] will redeem me unharmed
> from the battle that I wage,
> for many are arrayed against me.
> Psalm 55:16, 18

> For [God] did not despise or abhor
> the affliction of the afflicted;
> [God] did not hide his face from [her],
> but heard when [she] cried to [God].
> Psalm 22:24

The psalmist is telling us God has promised to be there, to hear our cry, not to desert us, no matter what. Can this be true?

Not only will God be present, says the psalmist, but there is judgment on those who bring terror and suffering, who break their convenants—and a word of prediction:

> But you, Oh God, will cast them down
> into the lowest pit;

> the bloodthirsty and treacherous
> shall not live out half their days.
>
> Psalm 55:23

So it was with Roy Alaniz, a man of blood and treachery. He did not live out half his days.

✳   ✳   ✳

We have here a tragedy, lived out for seventeen years and extended for perhaps another ten—yea, even unto the next generation, as the Alaniz children are now deprived of their mother.

Delia and her children lived with fear every day in their home.

Some of us have some idea of what Delia has lived through, although few of us could compare our experiences to hers.

For those of us who, because of gender, race, class, sexual orientation, or age, are vulnerable to violence, fear is a constant companion.

I would assume that there is not a woman here today who has not felt the fear of physical or sexual attack; some carry the memory as well.

There are many of us who as children felt fear in the threat of a bigger, older kid or of an abusive parent.

For a person of color, the fear that grips one's stomach when walking down the street and encountering a group of young white skinheads is very real.

Fear is especially intense for some of us because we know that we are at a disadvantage. While anyone can be the target of violence, some of us are much more likely to have this experience simply because of who we are.

Howard Thurman, the black pastor and theologian whose writings convey profound insight into the human condition, observed: "When the power and tools of violence are on one side, the fact that there is no available and recognized protection from violence makes the resulting fear deeply terrifying." Again Thurman:

> Physical violence. . . need not fulfill itself in order to work its perfect havoc in [our] souls....Fear, then, becomes the safety device with which the oppressed surround themselves in order to give some measure of protection from complete nervous collapse.[2]

How do we protect ourselves? By accommodating our behavior in order to reduce our vulnerability to violence.

As women, it is second nature to us to check the back seat of our car before we get in; it is second nature to feel our heart race when we hear footsteps behind us; it is second nature to decline an invitation to an evening meeting because we are afraid to go out at night; it was second nature for Delia to feel her neck muscles tighten whenever Roy walked into the room.

We agree to limit our lives as an accommodation to fear. Not only did Delia limit her life, she tried every means available to protect herself. Leaving him, seeking shelter, calling the police, having him arrested, not having him arrested, getting a restraining order, calling on her family for support; you name it, she tried it. But still he came after her.

It is very easy in response to Delia's case to conclude that it is an extraordinary situation, a rare occurrence, and yes, it is tragic, but she knew before she had him killed that there would be serious consequences.

Well, it is not so extraordinary; there are many women facing the choice that Delia faced every day. There are many women who have tried every available means to stop the violence in their lives and yet it goes on. There are many women who have chosen to defend themselves and are serving life sentences in prison.

In fact, this could easily be you or I locked in maximum security at Purdy. If any one of us had chosen to defend ourselves and our children from an attacker, we could be serving a long sentence for that choice. You and I.

* * *

So where is God's promise to us? Where is God's promise to Delia? Where is God's promise to those who choose to protect themselves in the face of violence?

The book of Revelation is a somewhat peculiar place to look for God's word in all this, yet here we do find it.

In Revelation, we are given this powerful image of the great dragon pursuing the woman who had recently given birth; she is obviously very vulnerable. But God gives her the wings of a great eagle in order to escape the serpent who pursued her and poured forth water by which to drown her. The earth, scripture says, opened its mouth and swallowed the flood. The woman was safe; the dragon was angry and went off to continue his attack on those who bore witness to Jesus.

It is a very powerful image: God sends the woman the means to protect herself from the power of evil. And the earth itself is her mainstay, her protector.

Traditionally this passage has been interpreted as a grand metaphor of the church in its struggle with the devil, the church being the woman with the Christ Child and the devil being the dragon, with God finally saving the church.

Let me suggest a slightly different metaphor here: I suggest that the woman represents women and the dragon represents violence against us. As we know very well, this dragon persists in brutalizing those who are seen as most vulnerable in our society, women and children.

Of course we must realize that the eagle's wings and the hole in the earth that save the woman do not defeat the dragon so that everyone lives happily ever after. The dragon goes elsewhere and directs his venom and misogyny at others. But God is very clear about where God stands in all of this.

God offers sanctuary to those who are vulnerable. God offers a safe place, a respite. God gives us the wings of an eagle; and the earth swallows up the efforts of our assailants to destroy us.

Perhaps we should pray for these: pray for an eagle's wings for Delia; pray for a great hole in the earth to swallow the system that continues to punish her for trying to protect herself and her children.

The role that God takes and the role that God expects of all of us is clear: it is to stand with, to be in solidarity with those who are vulnerable and threatened by violence and harm. It is to provide sanctuary and to seek justice.

What justice is served by a ten-year sentence for Delia? When she is released, her youngest child will be an adult. Her husband's violence deprived her children of a home free from fear; now the state will deprive these children of their mother, the one person who could help them heal from this trauma.

Now, I am sure that some of you are uncomfortable with the implications of what I am saying. I appreciate that. Ethically, this case raises the larger issue of self-defense. Whenever any one of us takes the life of another human being, we should be called to account for our actions. It is the accounting we give that matters. Self-defense is the accounting to be given in this case.

But there are two aspects of this as a self-defense case that are ethically troublesome for some people and involve subtleties that the law has difficulty grasping: premeditation and hiring a contract killer.

Supposedly, premeditation precludes self-defense. Legally one can only defend oneself if, *in the midst of being attacked*, one chooses to strike back and in doing so, injures or kills the attacker. This may be a reasonable view of an attack by a stranger. But it is unreasonable in understanding an attack by a husband.

The thing about wife abuse is that it is a series of assaults that take place over time, often increasing in severity. The victim knows the pattern well and knows the terrorism that her partner is capable of. She also knows that given her lesser physical strength and her fear of what her partner will do to her and her children, she is very unlikely to be able to stop him in the midst of an attack. The only way to stop his terrorism is to preempt his violence by striking before he can attack again.

And why didn't she do it herself? Most likely because she was so terrified of him that she knew she could never face him, even with a weapon in her hand. She agreed for someone who could to do it. An agent acted on her behalf.

When he sentenced Alaniz, the judge lectured her: "Our criminal justice system is not perfect, but it works." He told her she should have used it. She had used it and it had not protected her; now the system is punishing her for its own failings.

The killing of Roy Alaniz was not the failure of Delia Alaniz's moral character; it was the failure of our community. We, the community and the legal system, did not protect her from him. Even here, with the Domestic Violence Act, inadequate enforcement and too few social services to support victims mean that we cannot in fact guarantee the protection of battered women and their children from their batterers. Until we can, women will choose this last resort to end the violence in their lives.

They should be called to account for this choice. But they should not be punished for it.

There is something we can do for Delia Alaniz. We can ask the governor for clemency; we can ask him to commute her sentence to time already served. If you would like more information, see me after the service.

The prophet John believed that ultimately God would set things perfectly right: evil would be dethroned and righteousness exalted. As part of this process God asks for our help. We are the eagles' wings; we are the holes in the earth. It is for us to provide sanctuary, protection and justice. May God give us the love, the concern, and the means that we will need.

Let us pray: Spirit of the living God, who moves across the face of our hearts, open us to each other so that we might fully comprehend that when one of us suffers injustice, we all suffer injustice.

Make your presence real to us here today; may we taste it and feel it and hear it as it binds us one to the other. Move us and shake us to help bring an end to the affliction of the afflicted.

Use us as eagles' wings, as great holes in the earth, to bring safety and solace to those who live in fear.

Grant us courage and strength. Grant us your peace. Now and always.

Amen.

Notes

[1]Ed. note: Delia Alaniz was granted clemency by Governor Gardner on October 27, 1989, and had her sentence commuted.

[2]Howard Thurman, *For the Inward Journey* (San Diego: Harcourt Brace Jovanovich, 1984), p. 139.

PRAYING FOR THE WRATH OF GOD

Thomas G. Long

Then I heard a loud voice from the temple telling the seven angels, "Go and pour out on the earth the seven bowls of the wrath of God."

Revelation 16:1

A faculty colleague and I were being introduced recently to a visitor to our campus, a minister from a small town in a neighboring state. "This is Bob so-and-so," we were told. "He's the pastor of the Lutheran Church of God's Love." Greetings and handshakes were exchanged, and when Bob and his host moved along, my colleague leaned over to me and whispered, with a wink, "I wonder if across the street from Bob there's the Presbyterian Church of God's Wrath."

That quip evoked a gentle chuckle; the very idea that the Presbyterians, or anybody else for that matter, would name a church after something as somber as the wrath of God seemed laughable. After all, church names tend toward the more positive and upbeat dimensions of the faith: the Church of the Heavenly Rest, Grace Church, Prince of Peace Church—that sort of thing—not the Church of Righteous Judgment, or the Divine Vengeance Church, and *certainly* not the Church of God's Wrath.

In a deeper sense, the wrath of God is not simply an unlikely name for a congregation, it is also a theological *idea* we probably feel that we can just as well do without. Jonathan Edwards may have

---

Thomas G. Long is Frances Landey Patton Professor of Homiletics at Princeton Theological Seminary, Princeton, New Jersey.

roused and galvanized his hearers with his severe sermonic descriptions of "Sinners in the Hands of an Angry God," but today such dire messages seem fit only for the ragged tents of mill-village revivals and the hysterical Sunday-morning screamers who inhabit the right hand of the AM radio dial.

Moreover, the picture of a brooding, indignant, thunderbolt-strewing deity of wrath is incompatible with the larger, more enduring themes of the Christian faith: a God who is merciful and gracious, abounding in steadfast love; a Christ in whom all the promises of God find their "yes"; and a Holy Spirit who is the true Comforter of humanity. There may have been times in the past when people, fearful and guilt-ridden, felt that they had to join the Church of God's Wrath, but fortunately our understanding of God's grace has grown and matured, and we spend our Sundays in the cheery nave of the Church of God's Love.

What, then, can we make of this scene in the 15th and 16th chapters of Revelation? It is an account of the wrath of God in all of its sea-boiling, thunder-rolling, earthquake-rattling fury. Here we see the very kitchens of heaven serving up brimming bowlfuls of God's wrath to be poured by angels upon the face of the earth. And what we read is not just a *description* of the wrath of God; it is a hand-clapping, hallelujah-shouting *celebration* of its coming. This is a booming, robust sermon trumpeted from the pulpit of the Church of God's Wrath, and even those of us across the street, sitting in the pews of the Church of God's Love and singing "Gentle Jesus, Meek and Mild," can clearly hear its blast. Aside from closing our ears to it, what sense can we make of it?

Here's one suggestion for how we might see this text. Perhaps a passage like this one serves as a somber backdrop to help us see more clearly the grace of the gospel, just as the architecture of medieval cathedrals often included gargoyles lurking in the shadows to enable the worshipers to know how precious was the circle of light around the altar. In other words, maybe this text is a biblical version of Dickens' *A Christmas Carol*, a nightmarish Scroogian encounter with the Ghost of Armageddon Future, designed to enable us to wake up with relief, thanksgiving for the grace of daylight, and moral resolve to live a life of charity. It is true; we need occasional reminders of the judgment of God, which is graciously withheld even though it is what we deserve, to renew our delight in God's mercy, which comes as an unmerited gift. Mercy, after all, can be taken for granted, viewed too lightly, or even casually demanded as a right. As essayist Annie Dillard once observed:

The higher Christian churches—where, if anywhere, I belong—come at God with an unwarranted air of professionalism, with authority and pomp, as though they knew what they were doing, as though people in themselves were an appropriate set of creatures to have dealings with God. I often think of the set pieces of liturgy as certain words which people have addressed to God without their getting killed. In the high churches they saunter through the liturgy like Mohawks along a strand of scaffolding who have long since forgotten their danger. If God were to blast such a service to bits, the congregation would be, I believe, genuinely shocked. But in the low churches you expect it any minute. This is the beginning of wisdom.[1]

So, maybe this passage from Revelation simply reminds us of the destruction that could—and should—have been, in order to refresh our gratitude for the divine kindness that takes its place. But, to be honest, that is *not* what this text is about. Search the text as much as you wish; you will find not a hint of hesitation in the divine hand of judgment, no patient stilling of the Godly wrath, no cry of heavenly repentance, "O how can I hand you over. I will not execute my fierce anger!" Indeed, this text presents itself not as a dire warning to be heeded, but as joyous retribution to be welcomed. The pouring out of the bowls of God's wrath upon the earth is called "great and wonderful. . . true and just." This is no backdrop; it is the main event.

All right, then, if we cannot see the text as an apocalyptic rendition of Dickens, let us make another attempt at understanding. Perhaps the wrath of God announced in this text can be seen as a gentle correction, the sort of discipline exercised by a caring parent. Like the slapping of a child's hand headed for a hot stove, the wrath of God poured out on the earth may be painful in the moment, but protective in intent.

This, too, is a cheerful reading of the text, but, candidly, it will not wash either. Make no mistake, the divine wrath announced here is no tiny slap upon the human wrist, no little spoon-sized dose of bitter medicine, a dab of castor oil to make the world feel better in the morning. To the contrary, there are seven bowls, the full and perfect number, of steaming wrath from heaven, bathing the earth in scorching fire. It produces not gratitude or praise, but destruction, anguish, and curses.

We need to face the fact that this text will not be domesticated, and its harshness cannot be mellowed. It is what it appears to be: an unvarnished description of the wrath of God, poured out in full measure upon the earth. The only way—the only possible way—that we can faithfully hear it is to recognize both what it says *and* something of the circumstances of the people to whom it was said. We do not know many details about the first readers of Revelation, but we do know for certain that they were Christians undergoing excruciating duress, probably persecution by the civil government. They were believers in the God of life; they were paying for their faith with their lives. They trusted the God of justice; they were being convicted all the day long in the court of violence. They had put on the white robes of baptism; those robes were stained with the blood of oppression. They longed to see the face of Christ; they were condemned to gaze into the vicious face of evil.

They had no power, no resources, no friends at city hall. They had only promises, hymns, and prayers. And so they repeated again the promises: "I am the Alpha and the Omega,...who is and who was and who is to come, the Almighty." And they sang again the hymns: "You are worthy, our Lord and God, to receive glory and honor and power." And they prayed again the prayers: "Come, quickly, Lord Jesus." But what are promises if they remain unfulfilled? And what are hymns if they are whistling in the night? And what are prayers if they are prayed into the void of an Eternal Uncaring?

August Wilson's play *Ma Rainey's Black Bottom* takes place in a run-down recording studio in the Chicago of the late 1920s. Several black musicians have gathered to record with Ma Rainey, the legendary blues singer. As they wait for the arrival of Ma and rehearse their music, the musicians exchange conversation that slowly exposes the bitter racism of the world in which they live and the rage and self-hatred it breeds.

At one point Cutler, the band leader, tells the story of an incident that happened to a black preacher named Reverend Gates. Gates, it seems, was on a train from Tallahassee to Atlanta to visit his sister, who was ill. The train stopped at the little town of Sigsbee, Georgia, and Gates stepped off the train to use the bathroom. The bathrooms, however, were for whites only, and Gates was sent to an outhouse two hundred yards behind the station. While he was there, the train pulled out, leaving Gates alone in this strange town.

As Gates stood on the station platform wondering what to do, nightfall approaching, he noticed a group of white men gathering at the station, watching him ominously. Fearful of their intentions, Gates began walking down the tracks, away from the station, not knowing where he was going. The white men began to curse and taunt him; a gun was fired into the air. Gates stopped walking, and the gang of whites circled around him. He told them that he was Reverend Gates and that he was traveling to see his sister, who was sick. "Yeah...but can you dance?" one of them replied. Then the men tore the cross from Gates's neck, ripped his Bible into shreds, and forced him to dance. "That's the only way he got out of there alive," said Cutler, "...was to dance. Ain't even had no respect for a man of God!"

At this point, one of the other musicians, Levee, angrily responds, "What I wants to know is...if he's a man of God, then where the hell was God when all of this was going on? Why wasn't God looking out for him? Why didn't God strike down them crackers with some of this lightning you talk about to me?"[2]

When those words are uttered in the play, the silence of the audience becomes palpable. For some it is the silence of shock, for others the silence of shame or rage. For many, shock and shame and rage find their way toward silent prayer, "Don't let it always be this way, O God. Don't let all the evil mobs of blind hatred forever have their way with the powerless." Shame and rage, pain and hope, mingle together in a prayer of desperation: "Where the hell is God? O God, deliver us from evil! Where is God in this hell? Why isn't God looking out? Look out for us, O God! Why doesn't God strike down those who kill us? Where the hell is God? Come down, O God! Let justice roll down like the waters. Save us, O God! Come, quickly, Lord Jesus!"

It is in response to these cries that John speaks the word of our text. It is—and can only be rightly heard as—a promise from beyond all human time to the prayers of victims for whom the passing of time only confirms their fate and deepens their hopelessness. The God of the hopeless hears their cries and stirs in heaven. A loud voice from the temple says to the messengers of unyielding mercy, "Go and pour out on the earth the seven bowls of the wrath of God. Go to those places where human hope is held captive by cruel despair. Go to beds of pain where hungry death seeks another feast. Go to those places where racism, poverty, and greed will not relax their grip. Pour out upon the earth the wrath of God. Announce once more the liberation of Exodus, that God will set the people free and close the waters of the sea over all who pursue to destroy."

The problem with our understanding of the wrath of God is not that we have made too much of it, but precisely that we have made too little of it. Or, to be more exact, we have conceived of God's wrath in ways that are too small, too intrapersonal, too psychological. We have pictured a wrathful God as a larger version of a wrathful *us*—peeved, petty, and petulant. Because we are most wrathful when we are least loving, we have assumed the same to be true of God and have pitted the God of wrath against the God of love. Given the choice between these rival deities, no wonder we turn aside from the wrathful God in favor of the loving God.

To the contrary, though, to speak of God's wrath is to speak of God's liberating and redemptive love pitted against all that opposes it, all that would keep humanity captive and in slavery. God's wrath is that expression of God's love that will not allow victims to suffer everlastingly without hope, that will not forever abandon the helpless, that will not allow the forces that destroy and demean human life to speak the last word.

In Tillie Olsen's "I Stand Here Ironing," we overhear the troubled thoughts of an impoverished mother, standing at the ironing board and worrying about the note she has received from the school: "I wish you could manage the time to come and talk with me about your daughter. I'm sure you can help me understand her. She's a youngster who needs help ...." As she irons, this mother remembers her daughter's uneasy childhood and cries out, in her own way, for mercy:

> She was a child seldom smiled at. Her father left me before she was a year old....She was dark and thin and foreign looking in a world where the prestige went to blondness and curly hair and dimples, she was slow where glibness was prized. She was a child of anxious, not proud, love. We were poor and could not afford the soil of easy growth. I was a young mother, I was a distracted mother....My wisdom came too late. She has much to her and probably little will come of it. She is a child of her age, of depression, of war, of fear.

> Let her be. So all that is in her will not bloom—but in how many does it? There is still enough left to live by. Only help her to know—help make it so there is cause for her to know—that she is more than this dress on the ironing board, helpless before the iron.[3]

"Help her to know...that she is more than this dress on the ironing board, helpless before the iron." That is a cry, and a raging, and a prayer—a cry for mercy, a raging for justice, a prayer to the only one who can prevent the hot irons of evil from pressing down all hope and faith. The sad facts are that this mother and her daughter, and all like them, probably will not be spared the crushing weight of social brutality. From all the evidence at hand, the prayer will almost surely go unanswered, the heavens remaining coldly silent. The cruel forces of history will press and burn and destroy, and if we are left only with whatever hope can be squeezed from the circumstances at hand, we are of all people the most to be pitied.

But the word from the seer of Revelation is that God, who is not bound by the walls of history, will not leave the helpless forever alone. The prayers of all the hopeless have been heard, and neither death, nor principalities, nor things present, nor things to come, nor powers, nor height, nor depth, nor anything else in all creation can stay the hand of God's redemption. The Red Sea boils again, the earthquake shakes Golgotha once more, the heavenly courts are stirring, and Death itself, with all its arrogant allies, will be made to drink from the bowls of the wrath of God.

So, if you hunger for righteousness, hear this word of the wrath of God poured out on all evil. If you cry out in hopeless pain, hear this word of the wrath of God poured out on all foul disease and cruelty. If you cannot read the newspaper without weeping for children who are abused and war widows who grieve without consolation and people who starve with knots of grass in their stomachs, hear this word of the wrath of God poured out upon injustice. And pray—pray to God that it's true.

"Lord God the Almighty! Just and true are thy ways."

Notes

[1]Annie Dillard, *Holy the Firm* (New York and San Francisco: Harper and Row, 1977), p. 59.

[2]August Wilson, *Ma Rainey's Black Bottom* (New York: New American Library, 1981), pp. 95-98.

[3]Tillie Olsen, *Tell Me a Riddle* (New York: Dell Books, 1971), pp. 20-21.

DANGEROUS DOMESTICATIONS

Nancy C. Pittman

What are little boys made of, made of?
What are little boys made of?
Snakes and snails and puppy dog tails,
And such are little boys made of;
What are young women made of, made of?
What are young women made of?
Sugar and spice and all things nice,
That's what young women are made of.[1]

When I was growing up and hearing these words all the time, I was relieved that I was not "snakes and snails" and glad to be identified with "sugar and spice"! Not until my adult life did I become aware that this pervasive attitude about the niceness of good girls was a problem. What Robert Southey repeats in this seemingly innocuous poem is the age-old naming and domestication of the opposite sex, the other gender, woman. This simplistic division of humanity, no matter how attractive parts of it are, is a dangerous domestication. For not only has it been proven false, in that it doesn't reflect the true nature of women, and harmful, in its attempts to mold women into something they are not, but this attempt to tame a group of people also holds great danger—to women, to men, and to the church.

Nancy C. Pittman, a minister of the Christian Church (Disciples of Christ), is a doctoral candidate at Perkins School of Theology, Southern Methodist University, Dallas, Texas.

I have also learned well in my life that if girls are not nice, not sugar and spice, there is another name for them—a horrible name that, in the circles I traveled, was to be avoided at all costs. John the Revealer, in characterizing a deeper reality about human community, draws a familiar picture of the bad girl in chapter 17. It goes like this:

> Then one of the seven angels who had the seven bowls came and said to me, "Come, I will show you the judgment of the great whore who is seated on many waters, with whom the kings of the earth have committed fornication, and with the wine of whose fornication the inhabitants of the earth have become drunk." So he carried me away in the spirit into a wilderness, and I saw a woman sitting on a scarlet beast....

There in the wilderness the angel showed John a horrifying image of idolatry, lust, and greed. He saw a woman dressed in all the finery that humankind could fashion, purple and scarlet silks and satins, bedecked with gold, jewels, and pearls. She was adorned with everything that money and power could buy, but she was not beautified by her costume. Rather, she was tawdry and cheap. And she was drunk on "the blood of the witnesses to Jesus," says John.

As I read the text, I see in my mind's eye a rumpled figure with crooked lipstick in stained and torn party clothes; she stumbles drunkenly, unaware that, after the dance at which she wooed so many with her charms that proved so false and hollow, she is now alone in her drunkenness. She is the terrible culmination of the biblical symbol of woman as whore or harlot (in the RSV), signifying humankind at its very worst, its lowest form. Women, or all humanity for that matter, cannot sink much lower than this prostituting woman who has flaunted the rule of God and followed her own way. And throughout the centuries, deliberately or not, this picture of the harlot of Babylon has too frequently served as a portrayal of real women. Woman, in her vanity, fell prey to the serpent's deception in the beginning, leading us all to sin and misery; now, woman remains the definition of the sins of self-absorption, self-pride, and self-idolatry.

Miss Sugar and Spice, a figure that John knew just as well as he knew the harlot, is the exact opposite of this evil woman. For several chapters later the same angel, "one of the seven angels who had the seven bowls," returns to John to show him the nice girl. "Come," the angel says, "I will show you the bride, the wife of the Lamb." And John records, "In the spirit he carried me away to a great, high mountain and showed me the holy city Jerusalem coming down out of heaven from God."This figure is "prepared as a bride adorned for her husband"; she is wondrously beautiful and radiant with the glory of God.

Of course, in American society of the twentieth century, we cannot help but see a young woman dressed in spotless white, an ethereal vision of filmy tulle, delicate lace, and soft satin, held together with tiny seed-pearls. Veiled from the cares and claims of the world, she is chaste and pure—virginal in her refusal of other suitors, cleaving only unto her betrothed. She is as passive as a mannequin, modestly waiting to receive the attentions of her husband. Moreover, she is the ideal of femininity, the essence of feminine pulchritude and virtue, and her portrait has been used to describe women as they might be—if only they were not so much like the harlot.

So John offers two pictures, polar opposites, which have symbolized our culture's deepest understandings about the nature of women. And we don't have to look very far to see that he is drawing upon prostitution and bridal imagery already present in the Hebrew scriptures and in Greco-Roman culture. For centuries, women have been either in the gutter with the harlot or on the pedestal with the bride. A friend told me recently of a bumper sticker he saw on the back of a pickup truck that said, "Fifty-one percent sweetheart; forty-nine percent bitch—Don't Push It!" What that woman had so succinctly captured in her bumper sticker was this ancient and abiding polarity—woman is either a bitch/harlot, or a sweetheart/ bride. The enduring vitality of this dichotomy in modern life is underscored by the depiction of the jealous lover and the faithful wife in the movie *Fatal Attraction*, or of the Sea Witch and Ariel in the Disney film *The Little Mermaid*.

If a woman is overly independent and self-reliant, if she has insisted on her own way too often and too loudly, if she has refused to bow her will to the accepted order of things, other words, besides *harlot*, will do. Hurricanes, the very definition of irrational destruction, were until very recently always given feminine names. Yet does the opposite pole, the "bride," provide a better image of women than that of the "harlot"? Hardly, though we know quite well the dimensions of this figure. She is the virtuous, but charming, girl, the submissive wife, the adoring and adored mother, the quiet and attentive widow. A woman as "bride" does not speak unless spoken to, and then only in low and carefully modulated tones; she does not doubt or question the men around her, and she serves in her world with silent and unassuming grace. She is a fair princess, a genteel and noble queen, a pretty doll, a sweet angel. She is not, however, a real human being with needs and desires, hopes and dreams, the ambivalent mixture of good and evil that characterize human beings. And while the harlot is manifestly, aggressively self-absorbed, this cultural image of the bride is totally self-less, lacking personality of her own, abdicating all claim to her own creativity and will.

Neither image, that of the harlot or the bride, gives us a fair description of the nature of women or the roles they should assume in the community of the faithful. In fact, they are dangerous in their stubborn insistence that people be stereotyped into categories that do not fit. So what are we to do with this troublesome imagery in John's Revelation? Do we not, at the very least, acknowledge his participation in the sexism of his time and our own complicity in transmitting them? Yes. Then do we throw out these texts as inappropriate and useless? No. We cannot allow the medium to obscure the message. We cannot allow these persistent domestications to impede a more appropriate and faithful interpretation of John's text, particularly of his bridal imagery.

John, you see, has something profoundly true to say to us about what it means to be in human community away from God—and with God. Sometimes the community is idolatrous, choosing its own ways instead of God's ways and exalting itself as the highest and best instead of God and God's grace. When we participate in this idolatrous community, which most assuredly all of us do at different times, we become the faithless one in John's text having no permanent partner, but seeking attendants who will tend to our needs blindly. At times, in our faithlessness, we scheme to involve as many others as possible in our plans for personal power and glory and we try to trap them in our worship, promising everything and giving nothing. At times, we seek to know others only insofar as we can gain from them. At times, we serve as our own shepherd, our own standard, and point only to ourselves as the ultimate in life.

But sometimes, in mystical, magical moments, the community is redeemed. Sometimes, through God's gracious love, we are lifted out of destructive preoccupation with ourselves and our survival, and become the true partner of Christ, the one that John tried to symbolize in his bridal imagery. In such sacred moments, we manage to love others as we love ourselves. We give up debilitating fears or lusts so that we might participate fully in the gospel and in the whole community of God's people, for the whole world. We stubbornly cling to the name of Jesus in the face of the claims of other gods. Through Christ Jesus we have been redeemed and our hope exists in living out that redemption in the world.

It is precisely at this point, as we seek guiding metaphors for the redeemed life, that our contemporary stereotypical image of the "bride" becomes totally useless either as a model for faithful women or for the redeemed Christian community. The bridal community that John envisions is not a self-abnegating, passionless being, passively waiting for someone else to complete her existence. No, John's bride is an active partner befitting the Christ who has given all on behalf of God's reconciliation to the world. The redeemed community, for John, is comprised of martyrs and saints who could not possibly be motivated in the fulfillment of their faith by either self-interest or masochistic self-renunciation. Rather, they are inspired by commitment to the Lamb of God to perform righteous deeds in the world on behalf of others, even unto death. Indeed, according to a hymn in chapter 19, the very clothing of the Bride is made up of those deeds, signifying the community's constant and diligent participation in the preparation for the final union between itself and Christ.

If the message is true, but the medium obscures its proclamation, then new images, new media, must be found to express the abiding partnership with Christ to which we are called. We must find more appropriate ways of naming ourselves and the energy, gifts, and qualities we bring to the church that are more true to the reality of a redeemed community. To date, such new or different images have not been claimed by our culture. Until they are, we can still see in the stories of real women new ways of describing our partnership with Christ.

Rebecca[2] grew up in a home where cruelty reigned, where horrifying abuse and neglect were the staples of her life. By way of coping with the terrible hurts that her mother and father inflicted upon her, she pretended that what her parents were doing to her was not really being done. As she grew up and moved away from them, her game of pretense became so real that she completely forgot the pain of her childhood. She married, had children, and set about the task of living life as Miss Sugar and Spice, sublimating so thoroughly what had happened to her as a child that she honestly believed her relationship with her mother and father had always been good and healthy.

Cracks began to appear in the facade of Rebecca's life, however. Her marriage to an abusive man crumbled, her skills as a parent were minimal, at best, and her self-concept as an adult woman fell apart. The horror of her childhood finally reared its ugly head as she began to remember what had happened. She also recognized what had been the basic component of her self-image for as long as she could remember: "I am bad and I deserve the pain inflicted upon me by my parents, by my husband, by life." In order to cover up what she believed to be her true evil nature, she had made every effort to be Miss Sugar and Spice all her life.

In desperation she sought the help of another woman, a pastoral counselor. And in their time together, Rebecca began to learn, at the deepest level of her being, the real truth, that she was unconditionally loved by God. What had happened to her was absolutely not her fault; moreover, whatever sins she had committed in her short life were nothing compared to the redemption offered through Jesus Christ. At last, she was able to reject the ugly name that her parents had called her as well as the falsely pretty name that she had so vainly tried to achieve. And she literally renamed herself. Through the courts, she took a new first, middle, and last name to reflect intentionally her true identity as a beloved partner of Christ, as a member of the redeemed community.

In the months and years since her renaming, this woman has learned to be a wiser and more loving mother, a self-reliant person who can physically and emotionally support her family, a faithful member of the church, a healer of hurts in the world. She embodies the meaning of faithful partnership with Christ, forgiven, slowly and painfully forgiving, participating in the reality of Christ's redemption for the world.

What are young women made of? Not sugar and spice, and not wicked harlotry. No one, not even John, can make those dangerous domestications stick any longer. For women, like men, are made of blood, sweat, and tears, of the ambivalent mixture of goodness and badness that defines human living. Beneath John's faulty images lies the real truth: all of us, no matter what we are named, are called to be faithful members of the community that seeks to be Christ's partner in the world. Let it be so. Amen.

Notes

[1]Nineteenth-century nursery rhyme, attributed to Robert Southey, but not to be found among his works.

[2]Not her real name.

18

THE VIEW FROM THE MOUNTAINTOP

James E. Altenbaumer

I don't know what will happen now. We've got some difficult days ahead. But it doesn't matter with me now. Because I've been to the mountaintop. And I don't mind....I just want to do God's will. And He's allowed me to go up to the mountain. And I've looked over. And I've seen the promised land. I may not get there with you. But I want you to know tonight, that we, as a people, will get to the promised land. And I'm happy tonight. I'm not worried about anything. I'm not fearing any man. Mine eyes have seen the glory of the coming of the Lord.[1]

Martin Luther King, Jr. energized a generation with his visions of the promised land. Each time he told us his visions and his dreams of the America that could be, we were empowered to stand up against evil one more time and to give our witness to a future where hatred will not rule.

At the end of the first century of the Christian era, another prophet saw visions of the future. He felt oppressed by the society around him. His people were suspected because of their exclusive claims and behavior. They were rejected in their missionary efforts. He felt the fatal magnetism of the empire that drew away the wealth

---

James E. Altenbaumer is pastor of The St. John United Church of Christ in West Alexandria, Ohio, and a doctoral candidate at Candler School of Theology, Emory University, Atlanta, Georgia.

of his land to maintain imperial luxury at its center.[2] He and his people felt the pull to give up and give in, to accept the world of the day and to live in it. But in his vision he saw a new world, a future where his people would no longer be the object of fear and hatred, and where the evil empire would no longer sap the wealth of the world.

The prophet's name was John, and in the book of Revelation he hands on what was revealed to him. In chapter 18 John sees the end of the chief troublemaker, the fall of the great city Babylon, which most commentators understand to be Rome. And the vision makes it possible for him and his people to resist and to rejoice.

The vision is reported in songs, very different songs. Those who had profited at Babylon's coattails sing sad songs, while angels' songs announce the judgment and call for celebration. The tension between these two groups of songs raises the two great questions of this chapter. Why is it sad that evil Babylon has fallen? And why, in light of that, is it time to rejoice? Through this tension, the vision of God's new world becomes clearer: pain and joy at the wonder of it all. Like childbirth. Like the cross, where "sorrow and love flow mingled down." In truth, like all the great pivotal experiences of life where, sadly and joyfully, we say good-bye to what has been and turn our faces to what is to come. If we hear only the sad songs of all that's lost, we end up living in the past. If we hear only the joyful songs of the future, we ignore the very real sense of loss we are feeling. No, like John and his people, we have to hear both songs.

"Fallen, fallen is Babylon the great!" cries an angel with a mighty voice. Her pride and power are stripped away. Her streets are empty. Her lackeys—kings, merchants, and seafarers—mourn her from afar. Each group raises its voice to express the great loss. Three times their songs begin: "Alas! alas!" The kings, who ruled their provinces only at Babylon's pleasure; the merchants, who grew rich because of the peace that she maintained; and the shipmasters and sailors, who profited from every load of cargo—each in turn mourn her fall.

"No great loss," we may say, when our enemies fall. And yet for John the fall of Babylon must have been a great loss, because he has included these laments. Some find a poignant sense of loss in these verses—in a sense the mourners speak for John as well as for themselves. "He has had to be told not to stare in wonder at [Babylon] the great whore (17:6–7), for he too was able to appreciate the glamour and brilliance, however deeply aware he might be of their dangers."[3] John did not simply reject material goods; in a later vision he sees the holy city filled with them. "There was nothing sinful about the commodities which made up Rome's luxury trade, until the great whore used them to seduce mankind into utter materialism."[4]

But regardless of her splendor, Babylon has fallen. In earlier visions we have witnessed John himself (1:17) as well as heavenly beings (5:8; 7:11) falling in worship before God, but Babylon has never taken part. Now she too has fallen before God. Beginning with that play on the word *fall*, John offers us a whole series of contrasts between Babylon and God. God "lives forever and ever" (1:18; 4:9); but Babylon, who had considered herself immortal, sees her end come "in one hour" (18:10, 17, 19). All the heavenly creatures gave glory to God and to the Lamb; but Babylon had glorified herself (18:7). While God's servants offered praise to God, the kings and merchants and sailors went after Babylon; but now they abandon her and their praise turns to sorrow: "Alas! Alas!" In God's new city, death, mourning, crying, and pain are no more (21:4); but in Babylon music and crafts and commerce and the joy of the wedding are no more (18:22–23). All these are "no longer in her" because of what *is* in her, "the blood of prophets and of saints, and of all who have been slaughtered on earth" (18:24).

Let's think about it. Babylon was rife with sin and had to go. No doubt about it. As tempting as Babylon's splendor was, it covered a core of "impure passion" and "wanton fornication." Babylon had deceived all the nations with her power and splendor (18:3 RSV). The fall fit the crime. And yet it is sad, because Babylon was truly splendid. William Stringfellow looked at America in the 1970s as John did at Rome in the late first century and intoned his lament: "Babylon is the story of every nation and, right now, is a parable for America."[5] Like John, Stringfellow believed that America deserved its fate and that our hope, finally, must be in God and not the nation. But all of us have to admit that, were America to fall like Rome and like Babylon, it would be a time for songs of great sadness.

This brings us to the second question: why does John call us, in the midst of this lamentation, to rejoice? John's vision lays bare the cruelty and pain that support Babylon's splendor. But the vision also transports his people from the oppression they feel to the mountaintop, so that they too can look into the promised land. John's vision of the future empowers his tempted and embattled people in the present: "Rejoice over her, O heaven, you saints and apostles and prophets! For God has given judgment for you against her!" (18:20). John's vision assures them "that though the wrong seems oft so strong, God is the Ruler yet."[6] And it's time to rejoice.

When someone asked Nietzsche what Christians would have to do to convince him of the faith, he replied, "They would have to sing better songs to make me believe in their Redeemer."[7] This is exactly what John was saying to his people. God's future is coming. The past is being swept away. Sing better songs!

Can John's vision empower us in the way that Martin Luther King's visions did? Can John's vision of the future grip us in a way that will energize us, a way that will enable us to step away from and resist the powers that seduce us? Can John's vision help us to sing better songs? What does Revelation 18 offer us?

Down there in the valley, Babylon overwhelms us with her splendor and her power—how can anyone resist her? But up here on the mountain with John, we can look over Babylon's head; we can look past the long and difficult journey and view the promised land. And with that vision we can rejoice.

Down there, we get caught up in a nationalism that runs off in any direction to defend our way of life. But up here, we see a finer vision of God's realm. To lose our way of life would be sad indeed; but what great joy to find God's way!

Down there we run with the rest of the pack in the rat race for self-fulfillment. Up here, we see a vision of God's new community, in which the water of life is free. To drop out of the race would sorely disappoint us; but, oh, the joy of that heavenly fellowship!

Down there, the church models itself on the society and strives to become bigger and better. Up here, we see a people married to the Lamb, devoted to the Lamb who was slain. To see an end to all our efforts to grow for God would break our hearts; but what wonderful joy to share that intimacy with God!

The vision sees beyond the attraction of Babylon. Some of us may not want to look. We enjoy the triumphs of our nation, our selves, our church. Down there, in Babylon's world, we can see nothing greater than her splendor, and we long to be like her. But up here, on the mountain, we share John's vision and realize that we have been seduced. We may not want to see it. We may be so enthralled by Babylon's glitter and delusions of grandeur, that we turn away from the vision and join in the laments: "Alas, Babylon!"

But if we stick with it, we hear the call of God:

> Come out of her, my people,
> so that you do not take part in her sins,
> and so that you do not share in her plagues.
> Revelation 18:4

Maybe John wants his people to withdraw physically, to have as little to do with the culture as possible. In our day we see some who take the command literally and dissociate themselves from all that's worldly. In *Christ and Culture*, his classic analysis of the relations between Christianity and civilization, H. Richard Niebuhr called this stance "Christ against culture." For Niebuhr this radical, exclusive position is necessary but inadequate. It is necessary, because "every Christian must often feel himself claimed by the Lord to reject the world and its kingdoms with their pluralism and temporalism, their makeshift compromises of many interests, their hypnotic obsession by the love of life and the fear of death."[8] It is inadequate, because "it affirms in words what it denies in action; namely, the possibility of sole dependence on Jesus Christ to the exclusion of culture."[9] We cannot escape culture.

Maybe John wants his readers to fly off to an isolated wilderness somewhere. But I don't think so. Why should we read this verse literally when so little else in the book can be read that way? If we took the call to come out less literally and more creatively we would reassess our values and our means of acquiring security—whatever form that acquiring takes. We would look long and hard at the powers that fascinate us and prompt our allegiance. And so we might resist being seduced.

However we read the call to come out, the vision issues a second call: the call to celebrate a reality not dominated by Babylon. Is there some spiteful glee here? Is John glad that Babylon has received just what she deserved? Or is John as sorry for the fall of Babylon as the kings, merchants, and seafarers? Probably neither. I watched with the rest of the world as East Berliners poured through the Wall. I saw no vindictiveness there, only euphoria. I sense the same emotion in John's vision. Yes, Babylon got what she deserved, but it was simple justice that had to come. Babylon's fate simply fades out of the picture before the joy of the vision and the invitation to sing better songs.

We preachers often moralize too much about what we should do and celebrate too little what God has done in Jesus Christ. From the beginning John has assured his people that they have been set free: neither seduction nor persecution can rule those who keep the faith. The blood of the Lamb has freed us from our sins (1:5) and purchased us for God (5:9). The Lamb is absent from the vision of Babylon's fall, but his faithful ones, the saints and prophets, act on his behalf. Their own blood now stains the streets of Babylon and bears witness to the blood of the victorious Lamb. And it is time to rejoice. The vision confirms the end of Babylon's assault and the certainty of the judgment against her (18:20). And it's time to rejoice.

John has stood in the heavenly court and seen God enthroned in power. John has been to the mountaintop and seen the ultimate outcome. John has heard the verdict and shown us the end of Babylon. John calls us to endure patiently and to witness faithfully, but also to discern carefully, in the certain knowledge that we shall overcome. As King said, "We've got some difficult days ahead. But it doesn't matter with me now. Because I've been to the mountaintop....And I'm happy tonight!" As we stand on the mountaintop with John and Martin, it's time to sing better songs. It's time to rejoice!

Notes

[1]Martin Luther King, Jr. Speech, 3 April 1968. Memphis, Tennessee.

[2]This paragraph follows A. Y. Collins, *Crisis and Catharsis: The Power of the Apocalypse* (Philadelphia: The Westminster Press, 1984), pp. 85-97.

[3]G. B. Caird, *A Commentary on the Revelation of St. John the Divine* (New York: Harper & Row, 1966), p. 227.

[4]*Ibid.*

[5]See William Stringfellow, *An Ethic for Christians and Other Aliens in a Strange Land* (Waco, Tex.: Word, 1973), pp. 32-33.

[6]M. D. Babcock, "This Is My Father's World."

[7]F. Nietzsche, *Thus Spake Zarathustra*, cited in Hans Kung, *The Church* (Garden City, N.Y.: Image, 1976), p. 201.

[8]H. Richard Niebuhr, *Christ and Culture* (New York: Harper & Row, 1951; Harper Torchbook edition, 1966), p. 68.

[9]*Ibid.*, p. 69.

19

THE FINGER OF GOD

Allan A. Boesak

On the Information Scandal[1]

> And the magicians said to Pharaoh, "This is the finger of God!" But Pharaoh's heart was hardened....
>
> Exodus 8:19

> Then I saw heaven opened, and there was a white horse! Its rider is called Faithful and True, and in righteousness he judges and makes war.
>
> Revelation 19:11

According to the church father Irenaeus, the book of Revelation was written at the end of the reign of Domitian, the Roman emperor who turned the tradition of emperor-worship into a law. Under him the worship of the emperor became a legal requirement rather than merely a custom. It is thus understandable that tension in the Christian congregations increased at that time. The struggle between the Kyrios, Jesus the Messiah, and the temporal ruler, the emperor, became more pointed than before.

Allan A. Boesak, a minister of the Dutch Reformed Mission Church of South Africa, is former president of the World Alliance of Reformed Churches. This sermon was translated from the Afrikaans by Peter Randall and published in *The Finger of God: Sermons on Faith and Socio-Political Responsibility* (Orbis, 1982). It is reprinted with the permission of the publisher, for which we are grateful.

It is also understandable that proclaiming the word of God and professing Jesus as Lord frequently led to adversity. Can this be the reason—this continuing and sharpening clash between the Messiah and the emperor—why John, the minister of the congregation in Asia Minor, found himself in exile on the desolate island of Patmos, charged (was he ever formally charged?) and sentenced for proclaiming this "subversive" message: Jesus Christ is the Lord? (Incidentally, is it not noteworthy how totalitarian regimes since that time have shown a predilection for islands?[2])

However that may be, John is in banishment on the island of Patmos, apparently serving his sentence by command of the emperor. For him the conflict between Kyrios and Caesar has led to this point. But John knew and the congregation knew: precisely on this point the faith of the Christian congregation would have to prove itself. They would have to rise above their slave mentality and exchange their fear of the authorities for fear of the Lord. The conflicting loyalties were clearly spelled out: God or idol; Lord or emperor; Domitian the son of the gods, or the Son of God. Which name would be avowed?

John is now on the island: offender, subversive, agitator, outcast.

But—and this is really tremendous—he is not there alone! God himself is keeping him company. And it is about these endless, wonderful colloquies with his God that John tells us in his writings. But there is even more. God not only talks with him. He lets John *see* as well. And not only that: he is allowed to see *what God sees*.

John Sees What God Sees.

In the 19th chapter, John is describing what he sees: "Then I saw heaven opened...." This time it is not, as in Revelation chapter 4, a door that is opened, but heaven itself. God does not merely give John a glimpse. God sweeps aside the whole curtain. Nothing is withheld from John's view. He is allowed to experience this moment in its fullness.

What does he see, this banned person? He sees the rider on the white horse, he sees the triumphal entry of the Messiah. This time the Messiah is not imaged in the form of a lamb, mute before its shearers and led without resistance to the slaughter. This time John sees the hero on a white horse. The king. The prince before whose majestic visage the glory of the idolatrous emperor will pale to the tawdry glitter that it really is. This time he does not enter on a head-hanging, hollow-backed little ass. No, this time he is mounted on a charger.

The Lord of Lords

And his name—this is something that John cannot speak enough about in this chapter—his name is Faithful and True.

What kind of name is this? What other than *the* name! The name that he received after his victory over death and the forces of hell, the name above all other names. It is a name that recalls *the* name: the echoes of the first announcement of the divine name sound clearly here—*I am what I am.*

The firmness and the truth of this name had been discovered by Israel centuries earlier. He is what he is, he will be what he will be, in his association with his people, in the struggle with the pharaoh, in the emancipation from slavery, in the long, long trek through the desert. In the words of the prophets, in Jesus of Nazareth—in all this he showed that he had the power to do as he promised, to keep his covenant. So he is called Faithful and True, and now too he will do as he has promised, as he did before.

Presently John will say that only the rider himself knows his name (19:12). But then John whispers the name in our ears: "The Word of God" (v. 13). Eventually John will be able to contain himself no longer and will jubilate: the name is "King of kings and Lord of lords" (v. 16). *That* is what he is! And the kings of the earth? He is the king! The lords of the world, indeed!—those who call themselves *baas* ("massa").[3] *He is the Lord!* Who still bows down before Domitian? Who is still afraid of the pharaoh?

The pharaoh, like the emperor, was a son of the gods. Like the emperor, he too was worshiped. He was like a god, with power and status, this man who for so long decided the fate of nations, including that of the people of God. By the time we come to Exodus 8, he had absolute rule over Israel and he denied God's people the destiny that Yahweh had in mind for them. He had decided that God's plan for them would be foiled, because, after all, who was this God? "Who is the LORD?" the pharaoh asked scornfully. "Who is the LORD that I should heed him?" (Exodus 5:2).

God wished his people to be freed, to become *his* once again. The pharaoh refused. And he refused not only because he thought he had the power to do so but also because he knew that God's liberating action for his people would mean the end of his own rule. On the grounds of his power and his continued rule he made his decision; he refused. Now, however, he had to take account of the power and the rule of the living God.

Hence the plagues. Little by little the undercutting of the pharaoh's rule. Ten times came the challenge. The continual undermining of his power, the exposure of his impotence, and eventually, the public display of his insignificance. When the living God lifts his finger, the nakedness of the powerful is revealed. After the pharaoh, the baals and the dragons would discover the same thing. Even though there were seven plagues still to come, even though the earth would still have to become a valley of death before the pharaoh would give up the struggle, already he, the anonymous antigod of Exodus, was hearing from the mouths of his magicians: it is the finger of God!

This admission (in spite of themselves!) was made at this stage only by the pharaoh's magicians—the ideologues of the Egyptian court, the strategists of his propaganda, the inventors of the secret weapons with which he expected to defeat Israel and the God of Israel. They were the brilliant party conjurers, specially trained always to be one jump ahead of the others. They were the ones who had to realize, with great frustration and remorse, that their magic tricks no longer worked. They could only add one problem to another. They could aggravate the problem, but they could not solve it.

It was at this point that they realized with astonishment: "This is the finger of God!"

For the pharaoh himself it was still obscure, but it was soon to become clear to him also: "By this you shall know that I am the LORD..." (Exodus 7:17).

Note well that this is the same pharaoh who shortly before had said: "I do not know the LORD" (5:2).

John sees it. The Caesar under whom the Lord's congregation was so heavily yoked would, despite all his power and glory, eventually have to admit that Jesus the Messiah is the Lord and more, that he is the victor.

And this victor would come to judge his enemies. No escape is possible. He judges and he wages war in righteousness. John leaves no doubt about the intentions of this victor-prince.

"His eyes blazed like fire," our translation reads, somewhat incorrectly. Literally it should be: "His eyes were a flame of fire." Once again the unequivocal, pictorial language of the Bible. It reminds us of the consuming fire from which Isaiah shrank back (Isaiah 33:14); the scorching flame of which Paul speaks and that will eventually test all human works (1 Corinthians 3:13).

For John it means that nothing is concealed from the Lord. He uncovers—in the sense of unmasks—everything. His eyes are a flame of fire—they burn with holy wrath and the fury of God, the almighty (Revelation 19:15b). And ultimately there is the sword—the sign of judgment and justice—that comes from his mouth to strike the nations.

So clear, fierce, and unavoidable is the judgment of the Messiah, the Lord of lords, the King of kings.

If his cloak is spattered with blood, it is the blood of his enemies, of the destroyers of his progeny, of the tyrants who with immeasurable arrogance dare to challenge the Kyrios. It is the blood of the pharaoh and his armies. Once again the Lord is the one whose finger is pointed in righteousness and judgment at the powerful who live on injustice.

The pharaoh, the baals, the emperor, the powers of today—they all see it eventually, the finger of God.

When Richard Nixon defeated Senator McGovern in 1972 it was one of the biggest victories by any politician in the history of the United States. President Nixon later interpreted it as a sanction or justification of his policies, policies that resulted in neglect of the poor in the U.S.A. itself and the escalation of the unholy war in Vietnam.

And there was something that passed almost unnoticed at that time. Just after the election a small book about McGovern's defeat appeared, with the significant title *Goodbye Mr. Christian*. For me it was the first indication of what could happen: this small book substantiated the thesis that it was not possible to practice Christian politics in "Christian" America. Was this book a pointing of the finger? I think so. And later there was the terrible Christmas of 1972 when the U.S.A. bombarded Hanoi in a manner in which even Nazi Germany had not acted during the Second World War. Then many others saw what the president did not wish to see: the finger of God.

Watergate was merely a "last judgment," unavoidable, inescapable.

What we have been reading in all the South African newspapers recently about the escapades of the department of information and its officials has all the ingredients of a large-scale scandal. But for the Christian it is more than this: it is the finger of God.

It must be said that blacks are not at all surprised at the revelations that men in high government positions use immoral methods to defend the policies of their government to the outside world. In a certain sense the department minister and his subordinates could not do otherwise. When a policy is immoral in its essence, when violence is inherent in a political system, what else can one expect but that it has to be defended by immoral means and an escalating cycle of violence?

And besides, laws that clash with the gospel of Jesus Christ, laws that degrade and deny the human dignity of entire stratums of a national population, that separate husbands and wives from each other, that trample underfoot the most elemental of human rights— did any of us really think that God would allow all this to go on without punishment? And just like the pharaoh's magicians, these officials now begin to understand that their magic tricks do not work. With all their busy little schemes and plans all they could do was heap up problems for themselves. They could solve nothing, merely add plague on top of plague.

But it will get worse. What is happening here is more than just a symptom of corruption in one government department. it is more than just an indication of the immorality of certain government authorities. It is much more than just the demoralizing exposure of the hollowness and the spiritual bankruptcy of a particular political policy. And at a deeper level it is the finger of God pointed at injustice and unrighteousness.

And it will get far worse. As did the pharaoh, government officials will harden their hearts and they will refuse to listen until the rider on the white horse appears. What we are seeing now is the beginning of God's judgment on those who have long-trampled his righteousness underfoot.

Believers see: this is the finger of God! But they see yet more: they see the rider on the white horse, the Lord, the Kyrios, the victor. It is he who rises above the powerlessness of his people and strikes the enemy with the judgment of his mouth. The people of God do not have to abandon their faith; they do not have to re- nounce the Messiah. Believers can be sure—despite the show of power and the sternness of the emperors of this world—that he is the Lord of lords, the King of kings.

And Jesus Christ is yesterday and today the same, and even unto eternity.

> After this I heard what sounded like the roar of a vast throng in heaven; and they were shouting: "Alleluia! Victory and glory and power belong to our God, for true and just are his judgments! He has…avenged…the blood of his servants." Then once more they shouted: "Alleluia!"
>
> Revelation 19:1–3, NEB

Notes

[1]In September 1978 it became public for the first time that the South African government's department of information had been using immoral means to "sell" the government's policy of apartheid to the outside world. Large sums of money were used to bribe persons in high positions, phony organizations were set up, attempts were made to purchase newspapers (such as the *Washington Star*). The present sermon was preached after the first week of newspaper stories on the subject. Revelations would continue for months. More than a year later the minister responsible for the department had to resign, the state president had to resign, and there were other momentous changes, all of which caused great confusion in the country. The corruption that was uncovered was a heavy blow to Afrikaner pride and "sincerity."

[2]In the South African context, the reference is to Robben Island and its infamous prison where the white government has imprisoned most of the black political leaders, among them Nelson Mandela, Walter Sisuiu, and the leader of SWAPO (South West African People's Organization), Herman Toivo ja Toivo.

[3]The Afrikaans word *baas* is generally translated "boss," but its full political and emotional impact is better conveyed by the old American slave term *massa*.

POETRY OF HOPE

David G. Buttrick

Then I saw a new heaven and a new earth; for the first heaven and the first earth had passed away, and the sea was no more. And I saw the holy city, the new Jerusalem, coming down out of heaven from God, prepared as a bride adorned for her husband. And I heard a loud voice from the throne saying,

> "See, the home of God is among mortals.
> [God] will dwell with them as their God;
> they will be [God's] peoples,
> and God himself will be with them;
> [God] will wipe every tear from their eyes.
> Death will be no more;
> mourning and crying and pain will be no more,
> for the first things have passed away."

And the one who was seated on the throne said, "See, I am making all things new....I am the Alpha and the Omega, the beginning and the end."

Revelation 21:1–6

And [God's] servants will worship [God]; they will see [God's] face, and [God's] name will be on their foreheads.

David G. Buttrick is professor of homiletics at The Divinity School, Vanderbilt University, Nashville, Tennessee.

> And there will be no more night; they need no light of lamp or sun, for the Lord God will be their light, and they will reign forever and ever....Amen. Come, Lord Jesus!
>
> Revelation 22:3–5, 20

There is a church in the Northeast with a stained-glass window problem. High above the chancel, set in glass, is a picture of the Holy City, the New Jerusalem, dipping out of clouds toward the earth. Some of the church members want to tear the window down: "It is," they claim, "too otherworldly." Well, perhaps they're right. After all, with air pollution, terrorism, and drugs, we've enough on our hands without hankering after some make-believe town in the sky. Perhaps like the stained-glass window, we should dump the book of Revelation and stick to the here and now. Yet, there's something about the vision that grips us: "And I saw the holy city, the new Jerusalem, coming down...from God....And I heard a loud voice...saying..., 'Death will be no more; mourning and crying and pain will be no more.'" What a wonderful vision.

✶ ✶ ✶

A wonderful vision! The vision speaks to our deepest longings. Is there anyone here would not wish an end to death and pain and crying? For we live in a world where pain is fact, where salty tears stream down every cheek, where the mortality rate still runs at 100 percent. Oh, we chirp our little optimisms. Some years ago a university professor announced, "Fear and sorrow are no longer major themes....There's a new confidence in human power to make life happy by...secular means." Of course he wrote those words before there were hostages in Iran, or an AIDS epidemic, before broken human beings tumbled out of an airplane over Scotland. So nowadays we are less confident. We know that fear and sorrow may be here to stay; that human life may well be cruciform. Yet, we can't help dreaming, dreaming of a day when everything will be right and bright and good and glad: "A new heaven and a new earth," that's the picture.

Of course there's more to the picture than mere escape from personal pain; *Revelation envisions a world at peace.* For the Holy City has many gates, and the gates stand open day and night. And through the gates shall stream kings and conquerors, nations and races, all joining together as children of God. Do you know the American primitive painting entitled *The Peaceable Kingdom*? It shows a lion lying down with a lamb, a barnyard cow and a grizzly bear nuzzling each other, while in among the animals children laugh and play. The picture's a little romantic for our tastes. Apparently the artist had never heard of the C.I.A., or drug lords dealing death in Columbia. Perhaps the lion and the lamb will declare a truce, but what about north and south Ireland, what about the Middle East? The fact is we live in a world of power politics, not in a zoological society! So at least the Bible is realistic; the Bible knows there can be no peace until national power—including American power—bows down before the throne of God. Then, and only then, will we see a new heaven and a new earth and a many-gated city of God.

Oh, by the way, *there's something missing in the vision.* Did you notice? There's something left out. In the Holy City, there will be no more churches—no temples, no spires, no pulpits, no preachers, no squeaky chairs in the fellowship hall, no solemn Bible study circles. The dream gets better all the time, doesn't it? Think of it, the church is the only organization on earth that cheerfully announces its own demise; we know we haven't got forever. Of course, we forget the fact. We go on building thick-walled churches as if we had forever. But we don't; we are not permanent. In God's great plan we're headed for a phaseout. For who will need churches when God is near at hand, or need preachers when everyone will know the Lord! "And his servants shall serve him, and they shall see his face, and they shall reign forever and ever." See the Holy City. A wonderful vision. It speaks to our deepest longings.

✳ ✳ ✳

A wonderful vision? Perhaps it's too wonderful. Bluntly, *perhaps it's too good to be true.* That's the Marxist complaint, and they have a point. For human beings can fall victim to their dreaming and lose track of here and now. You know how it works: promise people pie-in-the-sky, and they'll willingly go hungry; tell them of ivory palaces, and they'll put up with a ghetto; hand them resurrection, and you can nail them to a cross! Has this been the story of the black community in America for the past four hundred years? As long as African-Americans sang spirituals—"Swing Low Sweet Chariot," and "All God's Chillun Got Shoes"—they worked as barefoot slaves. But when the sweet chariot broke down, we got black power—and rightly so! For, listen: if our Christian faith is nothing but a pipe dream to con people into putting up with things as they are, then it's not faith at all; it's damnable. How does Bertolt Brecht sing?

> Ah the grass, oh the grass, will look down at the sky,
> And the pebbles will roll up the stream,

And we all will be good without batting an eye,
We will make of our earth a dream,
On St. Nevercome, Nevercome, Nevercome Day.[1]

Is Christian faith a mirage, that will nevercome, nevercome, nevercome at all? If so, then like the stained-glass window, let's tear it down, and settle for the hard reality of here and now.

Yet, we can't. *Dimly we know that human beings cannot live without hope.* Hope makes human life possible. If life is nothing more than a prison cell in which we twitch and squirm until an unseen executioner arrives, then what's the use? Struggle is senseless, striving vain. Without hope we are absolutely paralyzed. Albrecht Dürer has a famous woodcut. He pictures a woman sitting dejectedly on dry ground. In the distance is a city waiting to be built, and beside her is a box of tools for building, but she doesn't move. She has no hope. Without hope, nothing is possible and, therefore, nothing attempted. Maybe that's what happened to us in America. We dreamed an American dream. But then there were two World Wars, plus Korea, Vietnam, Watergate, Irangate, and sad Nicaragua. Now have we lost all hope of changing the world? We seem to be paralyzed, singing our cheerless theme song, "Sit Down, People of God, There's Nothing You Can Do," and labeling it neo-orthodoxy! Listen, without hope nations do perish. So do people. We cannot live without hope.

Of course, it all depends on what hope you have, on what kind of vision you cherish. The trouble with most of us at the tag end of the twentieth century is that our hopes have turned to dust. The Communist dream of a proletarian state and the American dream of a technological messiah, both have foundered on the hard fact of human nature. For what's the use of a utopian dream if we're stuck with the same old men and women? Can we abolish death if there's a death wish in us all, or put an end to pain when refined cruelty is a human invention? Perhaps that wise man Norman Cousins is right when he brands us "Obsolete," for while we have changed everything outside of ourselves, we have not changed ourselves. Unless we can be changed we'll dream a Holy City but end with death and pain and a warring of nations, everytime. "A new heaven and a new earth"? My God! What we need is nothing less than a whole new human race.

✳ ✳ ✳

Well, now do you see why the Holy City must come down from God? The city must come from God because we can't build it on our own.

And do you understand why the book of Revelation hears a great voice from heaven shouting, "See, I make all things new!"? Left to ourselves all we can do is remake the old, trade in the stone ax for the B-2 bomber (Whatever good it will do!). Left to our own devices we'll dream a Holy City and build Babel every time. But, "See," cries the voice of God, "I make things new!" Well, God better, because we can't. God must shape a new heart for loving and a new will for living, and a whole new humankind. "I'll tell you what I believe," says one of Arthur Koestler's heros, "I think a new God is about to be born!" Koestler has it backward. The Christian says, "I tell you what I believe; a new humanity is being born by the power of God." For Christians have seen the vision and have heard the great voice of God, saying, "I am making all things new"—a new heaven, a new earth, and a whole new humankind. A new people of God; that's what the Bible promises.

What's more, *now after Easter, we know what God can do*. After Easter we know God can raise out of death and pain and crying a new humanity. For what else was there at the cross if not the vision reversed: nations in conflict, religion corrupt, and the darkness and the pain and the woman crying and death. And, they did prevail. How does the old creed go?—"Crucified, dead, and buried." If that's all, then that's the end of Jesus Christ and of the human story as well. But the creed doesn't end at the cross; it goes on: "The third day he rose again from the dead," and with him all our human hopes. The resurrection means nothing less than God has power to overcome old chaos and dying, mass evil and humanity's impossible cruel streak, and to make something new—a risen Christ and a new humanity. Listen, the Easter message is not simply news of personal survival. (Could there be anything more tedious than to go on being us forever?) Easter is God's shout down through history, "See, I am making all things new!"

Now, do you want to know a secret? *Making new: that's what's going on in the world*; that's what's happening. The Holy City is not future perfect, it's present tense. (Check out the Greek verbs in the text!) Now the Holy City is descending. Now God is making things new. Right now God is wiping tears and easing pain and overcoming the power of death in the world. Now! There's nothing otherworldly about the vision; it's happening now in the midst of our worn, torn broken world. And, with eyes of faith, you can see it happening. Oh yes, it's a bloody world—thousands are dead in Central America and how many, many more in the Middle East. But there's a growing clamor for peace, not just among left-wing types, but among people of goodwill everywhere. And yes, it's an unjust world; the ghetto, like an angry wound, disfigures every city. But there's a rising cry for justice in churches where God's own militant Spirit moves. Of course, there are still men and women whose motto is "No change!" who would rivet every daybreak to the past, and they are God's enemies. But others, seized by hope, see the future God has planned, and believe. In one of Joyce Cary's wonderful novels, a half-mad artist, swinging from a high-hung scaffold, tries to paint a mural of the new Jerusalem on the wall of a condemned building. An image of the Christian vocation: to paint the new creation on a condemned world, knowing that though the world may pass away, the picture will come true by the power of God. "I saw the holy city, the new Jerusalem, coming down out of heaven from God....And I heard a loud voice from the throne saying, ...'See, I am making all things new!'"

✳ ✳ ✳

What about the church with the stained-glass window problem? "Too otherworldly," the people complained. Well, they decided to keep the window after all. For they discovered that through the years the glass had faded so that through the golden image of the new Jerusalem they could see the towers of their own town; one city seen through the vision of another. Call it poetry or what you will; we are meant to live in the world with a vision of God's promises, judging injustice with hard truth, but taking hope where hope is sure, and trusting the power of God that raised up Jesus. See, our God is making things new!

Note

[1]Bertolt Brecht, "Good Woman of Setzuan" in *Parables for the Theatre,* tr. Eric Bently (New York: Grove Press, 1948).

THEN THE GLORY

Jaroslav Vajda

Then the glory
Then the rest
Then the sabbath peace unbroken.

Then the garden
Then the throne
Then the crystal river flowing.

Then the splendor
Then the life
Then the new creation singing.

Then the marriage
Then the love
Then the feast of joy unending.

Then the knowing
Then the light
Then the ultimate adventure.

Then the Spirit's harvest gathered
Then the Lamb in majesty
Then the Father's Amen.

Then
Then
Then.

Jaroslav Vajda is a hymn-poet and a retired pastor of the Lutheran Church (Missouri Synod). He lives in St. Louis, Missouri. Vajda's hymn "Then the Glory"